LIFE BEGINS AT FIFTY

A Comedy in Three Acts

by

ARMITAGE OWEN

LONDON
SAMUEL FRENCH LIMITED

SAMUEL FRENCH LTD
26 SOUTHAMPTON STREET, STRAND, LONDON, W.C.2
SAMUEL FRENCH INC.
25 WEST 45TH STREET, NEW YORK, U.S.A.
7623 SUNSET BOULEVARD, HOLLYWOOD 46, CAL.
SAMUEL FRENCH (CANADA) LTD
27 GRENVILLE STREET, TORONTO
SAMUEL FRENCH (AUSTRALIA) PTY LTD
159 FORBES STREET, SYDNEY

MADE AND PRINTED IN GREAT BRITAIN BY
LATIMER, TREND AND CO. LTD, PLYMOUTH

MADE IN ENGLAND

LIFE BEGINS AT FIFTY

First produced at the Grand Theatre, Llandudno, on 14th July 1952, with the following cast of characters:

(in the order of their appearance)

ROBERT (BOB) ANSON	*Peter Jordan*
SALLY ANSON	*Margaret Austen*
PETER ANSON	*Ivor Earle*
VICTORIA ANSON	*Mary Lewis*
HETTY	*Madge Trevelyan*
GRACE STEVENS	*Barbara Miller*
ELIZABETH (BETTY) ANSON	*Mary Tisdall*
WILLIAM FITZMARREN	*Horace Wentworth*
HARRY BATEMAN	*Peter Morley*
JOHN YARDLEY	*Frederick Keen*

The Play Produced by HORACE WENTWORTH
The Setting designed and painted by GEORGE ETTWELL

SYNOPSIS OF SCENES

The action of the play passes in the sitting-room of the home of MRS VICTORIA ANSON, in a busy town in the North of England

ACT I

One evening in winter

ACT II

About a month later. Evening, almost eight o'clock
The CURTAIN *is lowered for a minute or so during the Act to denote the passing of time*

ACT III

A week later. Evening, half-past seven

Time—the present

ACT I

SCENE—*The sitting-room of* VICTORIA ANSON'S *home, a large, comfortable and rather old-fashioned house in the North of England. An evening in winter.*

The room is homely and lived-in, giving the appearance of having been furnished thirty years ago and not touched since. There is a door up LC *leading to the hall and a door* L *leading to the dining-room. The fireplace is in the* R *wall and there is a window up* R. *The main furniture consists of a sofa* R, *an armchair* RC *and one down* R, *a small table* LC *with two chairs, a desk down* L *with a chair, and a chair* R *of the door up* LC. *There is also an occasional table up* L *and a pouffe by the fireplace.*

(See the Photograph and the Ground Plan of the Scene)

When the CURTAIN *rises, the sound of a baby crying is heard off.* BOB *(ROBERT ANSON) is standing by the fireplace smoking a cigarette. He is a vigorous, business-like man of about twenty-eight, and appears at this moment to be annoyed. His wife,* SALLY, *enters up* LC. *She is about Bob's age, and is dressed very simply in a rather faded jumper and shabby skirt.*

BOB. Thank goodness that kid's stopped yowling at last. Have you managed to get him off to sleep?

SALLY (*sinking wearily on to the chair* R *of the door*) Yes, and I hope he stays asleep for a few hours.

BOB. That crying gets on my nerves. Why couldn't we have one that didn't cry?

SALLY. They all cry. It means they're healthy.

BOB. Then ours must be bubbling over with vim and vitality. All the same, when you've had a day at work and come back to this . . .

SALLY. I'm with the child all day. I have to stand its crying, I have to feed it, wash it, attend to it generally, and you come home and think you're a martyr because it cries a bit. I'll exchange jobs with you any time, Bob.

BOB (*moving up to Sally*) Sorry, dear, but I got a bit rattled. It's not just the kid, I suppose.

(SALLY *rises and moves down to the table*)

SALLY (*fingering a book on the table aimlessly*) All right. But I sometimes wonder if you're ever sorry Bill was born.

BOB (*moving down to Sally*) Good Lor', no! I wanted the child, and especially a boy. Why, it's going to be a lucky kid one day, managing director of Richard Anson and Co.

SALLY. I wonder . . .

BOB. What do you mean?

SALLY. Oh, never mind. I was only thinking I can't imagine anybody being managing director except your mother.

(BOB *makes a movement of surprise*)

By the way, Bob, I'll have to ask you for money. Sorry, but a baby does cost a bit more.

BOB (*fumbling in his pocket*) Hope you don't want much?

SALLY. A couple of pounds will do.

(BOB *takes out a notecase and draws out some bank-notes*)

BOB. I should think so, too. Money's going like water at present. We'll have to be careful, you know.

SALLY. A pound doesn't go very far today, Bob. Thank you. (*She takes the note from Bob*) I'll try to be most careful, and if you like I'll give you a careful account of how I spend this. (*She moves to the fireplace*)

BOB (*sensing her dangerous mood*) There's no need for all that, Sally. I'm only asking you to weigh up things and watch expenses.

SALLY (*flinging herself down on the sofa*) Expenses! I like that. You know perfectly well I don't buy anything unless it's essential. I've bought nothing for myself for months. I had intended asking you for money to buy a new coat, but I knew what the answer would be.

BOB (*moving to L of the sofa and leaning over the arm*) My dear, I'd buy you anything if we could do it, but we can't.

SALLY. My present coat is six years old, and it was quite a cheap one, so I'm not asking for the earth. (*She rises and stands with her back to the fireplace, facing Bob defiantly*) How your mother can tolerate my going around like this, I don't know, but perhaps she enjoys people saying, "That's Victoria Anson's daughter-in-law. Isn't she shabby?"

BOB (*moving down* C; *angrily*) Why bring Mother into it?

SALLY. Because she pays you, and if she pays you so niggardly that I have to go about in rags, then it's her fault.

BOB. My mother pays me a wage——

SALLY. A pittance.

BOB. —and expects me and my wife to live accordingly.

SALLY. Whilst she piles up money like a gloating miser.

(*The baby's cries off grow louder, and* SALLY *crosses quickly up* C. BOB *moves up to stop her*)

BOB. Let him squawk a bit. You know what Mother says—"let 'em cry themselves to sleep again," and she knows all about this baby business.

SALLY. Your mother knows a lot about everything, and if

bringing up Peter and you is a sample of her maternal side, I'm not very impressed. (*She pushes Bob aside*) So, if you don't mind, I'll go and attend to my child, even against your mother's theory.

(SALLY *exits up* LC.
    As Sally exits, PETER *enters up* LC. *He is slightly younger than Bob. He is ready to go out and is fumbling in his overcoat pocket for his cigarette-case*)

PETER (*pausing in the doorway*) Is that infernal kid crying again?
BOB. Yes, and it's going to cry a lot more for the next six months at least, so if you don't like it you know what to do—clear out.
PETER (*taking out a cigarette and lighting it*) That's just what I am doing. I'm going this very minute.
BOB. I mean—clear out altogether.
PETER. This is my home. (*He comes down* C)
BOB. I thought it was mine, but it isn't anybody's except Mother's. She's the only one who really lives here. Everyone else is allowed to be here; that's all it amounts to.
PETER. What's wrong with you tonight?
BOB (*moving* R *to the fireplace, and turning to face Peter*) Oh, nothing. Just facing up to something Sally mentioned. If you want to know, I'm sick and tired of being poor, never having more than an odd pound or so.
PETER (*moving to* L *of the sofa*) Er—talking of an odd pound, I was about to ask you to lend me one. I'm a bit stuck till the week-end.
BOB. So am I. Ask Betty.
PETER. No use. She never has any spare, and she won't touch the housekeeping money—says Mother would spot it right away. I've tried it. (*He moves a few steps towards Bob*) Come on, Bob, just a quid. I'm meeting Pauline, and I can't do the heavy with her on one and nine. (*He pulls out some loose change from his pocket*)
BOB (*taking out his notecase*) I'll lend you ten bob, and that's all. (*He holds out a ten-shilling note to Peter*)
PETER. Well, it's only half the request, but it helps. At least we shall keep sober on the contents of my pocket. (*He takes the note from Bob and puts it in his pocket*) Thanks, old boy. (*He moves* L *away from Bob*) This money business is a pest. Don't know when I'll ever get married.
BOB. Take my advice; if ever you do get married, clear out of this house and make your own home.

(*As* BOB *speaks*, SALLY *enters up* LC *and comes down* C)

SALLY. Very good advice, Bob. A pity you didn't do it.
BOB (*turning to Sally*) How could I? Mother would have us stay on here.

SALLY. Oh yes, I know all that. (*She moves* R *and stands behind the armchair* RC) Wasn't I present when she said she didn't want to keep you here simply out of a mother's selfishness, but because the house was big enough and it would save money? Instead of setting up another home we could all remain here and be just one big, happy family.

BOB. Yes, that's right, and there was something in it. It does save money . . .

SALLY (*moving up to the window and turning angrily to Bob*) Save money, save money! That's all your mother thinks about.

BOB. It does save money, all living together.

SALLY. Of course. She knew she'd have to give you three or four pounds a week more if we had our own home, and if Peter gets married, the same thing will happen to him. (*She moves down towards Peter*) So long as his bed holds two, your mother won't worry.

PETER. Now you mention it, it won't really hold two; well, not comfortably. It would be a bit of a squeeze, you know.

SALLY. Then you'll have to do some squeezing.

BOB. Look here, Sally, why get so bitter about it? (*He moves a few steps towards Sally*) I know it's not so easy for you and with the baby here, but what can we do?

SALLY. We started wrong. (*She sits in the armchair* RC) Living with in-laws doesn't work. Often it can't be helped, but with you it could. You've a mother rolling in money, and yet you agree to this kind of life.

BOB. But I couldn't afford to rig up a home of our own.

PETER. That's right, you know, Sally. He couldn't. Mother isn't exactly noted for generosity in the family. Look at poor Betty. She slaves and toils away as a blessed general servant, and just for board and lodging. No Union rates for her.

SALLY. Then it's high time you did something. Two brothers and a sister who haven't the nerve to say a word to their own mother, and accept lower wages than a labourer in your own works gets.

PETER. After all, we have a jolly nice home and plenty to eat.

SALLY. But nothing in your pocket.

PETER (*moving* C) Precious little, I'm afraid. (*He jingles the change in his pocket*)

(BOB *moves to the armchair* RC *and sits on the right arm*)

BOB. I can see your point, darling, and I can see Mother's. I suppose she thinks she's doing her share by giving us a decent home, as Peter says.

SALLY. Have you no wish to be independent? Do you think I want to bring up my child by permission of your mother, with her supervising? Would any outside man suddenly brought into your works do your job for your money?

BOB. Well, perhaps not, but it's rather different. I'm in the family. (*He rises*)

SALLY. Yes, and your mother gets cheap labour, and the same with Peter.

PETER. I say, this is the way they talk when they're going to strike. Do you think we should go on strike, Sally?

SALLY. It's up to you what you ought to do. Two grown men shouldn't need telling.

PETER. You think we should stick out for more money? I'm all for that myself.

SALLY. It's not only money. It's status, position. Look at Bob; twenty-eight, elder son of the sole owner of this very prosperous business, yet he has no position above that of a clerk. He should be managing director.

PETER. And I should be secretary at twelve hundred a year. Bob, let's get cracking! What about presenting a what-do-you-call-it—an ultimatum, to Mother.

SALLY. I can hardly see Bob doing that.

BOB. It's not quite so simple. For nearly twenty years Mother's had to be father and mother to us all, and on top of that she's taken charge of the business. In my opinion she's made a marvellous job of it.

SALLY. She's built up a most successful business, I admit.

BOB. And she's had to bring up three children——

PETER. —in her spare time, you might say.

SALLY. Very true—"in her spare time". The business has been everything with your mother—*that's* been a success.

BOB. And we haven't? Is that what you're thinking?

SALLY. To her you are still her little boys. She's got so used to running the whole show that she thinks of you two as infants, utterly incapable of controlling the business.

PETER. I believe you are right, Sally.

BOB. But isn't it natural? (*He moves down* R *and sits in the arm-chair*)

SALLY. Natural or not, it's about time she woke up to the fact that you should be treated as grown men. If you don't do something, she'll go on and on until she's ninety, at which time you'll be near seventy—then you might get a look in.

PETER. What a simply appalling thought! (*He moves above the table to the chair* L *of it*)

BOB. Don't talk such rot, Sally.

SALLY. All right. You'll see. Just let things go on as they are. Your sister isn't any better. She should have made a stand years ago. I know I would. You wouldn't find me sticking the life Betty does.

PETER. Oh, Betty's all right. She's happy enough.

SALLY. I wonder. You might be surprised if you knew what Betty really thought. Half the people in this town forget you have a sister. She's never seen, and with her looks and personality she could have been married years ago.

PETER. Good Lor', I never imagine Betty married. (*He sits* L *of the table*)

BOB. I don't think she ever dreams of it herself.

SALLY. Just like brothers! (*She rises*) Never think of their sister as an attractive girl; and she is, but she never gets the chance to show herself, thanks to your mother. I can't feel sorry for you two, but I do for Betty. She's about thirty, and yet she's treated like a kid of twelve.

BOB (*rising; irritably*) Never mind Betty. She can fight her own battles.

SALLY. But you can't fight yours apparently.

PETER. My dear Sally, we could go on indefinitely, but what's the point? You know what we're up against, Bob knows it, and I know it, and there we are.

SALLY. So you'll just do nothing? Is that it?

PETER (*rising*) Well, for my part, I'm afraid I'll have to push off. The dear Pauline gets restive if I'm late.

SALLY. Having a good time and squandering money on that nitwit of a girl won't get you anywhere, Peter. She's only a little gold-digger.

PETER. She'll have to be damn clever to dig any gold from my pocket tonight. Well, I'm off, see you later maybe.

(PETER *exits up* LC *with a wave of the hand*)

BOB. Sally, was all that talk necessary in front of Peter? (*He flings himself into the armchair* RC)

SALLY. Sorry if it upset you, but I've been wanting to say something for a long time, and I think Peter should know how I feel. (*She sits on the left arm of the armchair* RC) Don't you see, Bob, I want you both to realize that you're no longer children?

BOB. But Mother still thinks we are.

SALLY. I know, and that's what riles me. All mothers think of their grown-up children as if they were still fifteen. In a way, it's not your mother's fault, but yours, for not telling her that now you are men, and capable of men's work.

BOB. And ask her to give up controlling the business and hand it over to us? Is that the idea?

SALLY. Well, not so bluntly as that, but gently mention to her——

BOB. —that it's about time she stepped down from the high chair and made way? (*He laughs bitterly, rises and moves* R *to the fireplace*) Oh yes, I can see Mother taking that. Don't forget, my dear, she's not yet an old woman. She's hardly fifty, and a pretty young fifty, too.

SALLY (*rising and moving to* L *of the sofa*) I'm not asking you to put a pistol to her head. I only want you to remind her of your

position, and suggest that perhaps you could take some respon-
sibility away from her.

BOB (*sitting at the right end of the sofa*) But didn't I do that when
we were married two years ago?

SALLY (*sitting beside Bob*) That was two years ago, and you
haven't mentioned it since.

BOB. I can't see that there will be any difference now if I do,
but to please you I promise I'll have another word with her, and
you can put your own word in if you like.

SALLY. No fear! You'll fight alone. A daughter-in-law isn't
usually too popular in family conferences.

BOB. You know, Sally, Mother isn't half as bad as you make
her out.

SALLY. She's a marvellous business woman, I've always
admitted.

(VICTORIA ANSON *enters up* LC. *She is a well-proportioned woman,
not stout, but tall, attractive and good-looking, and appears younger
than her forty-nine years. She is dressed rather severely in a dark
skirt and a white blouse, and looks rather like a prosperous secretary.
She walks quickly into the room carrying some papers, glances at Bob
and Sally and goes to the desk down* L)

VICTORIA (*looking through the papers*) Robert, I'm afraid you'll
have to go and see Cartwright Brothers about that last order.
For some reason they're complaining, and I don't like complaints.
You'd better take a trip tomorrow and clear it up. (*She sits at the
desk*)

BOB (*rising*) Yes, Mother.

VICTORIA. And at the same time . . .

(*The baby's cries are heard off*)

Sally, is that child crying again? What amazing lungs!

SALLY (*rising*) I thought I'd settled it. He must have rolled
over on his back again.

VICTORIA. Don't go. Let him cry—do him good. A sign of
health. Never stifle a child's cries, unless it's really ill. Leave them
alone. The more you fuss, the more often they'll cry to attract
attention.

SALLY. If you don't mind, Mrs Anson, I'd like to go and make
sure for myself.

(SALLY *moves up* LC *and exits*)

VICTORIA (*with a quiet sigh; turning back to her papers*) Sally is an
impetuous girl. She goes rushing about unnecessarily and getting
flurried whenever that child cries. I don't know what she would
do with three young children, like I had when you were all tiny.

BOB. She's naturally anxious, Mother.

VICTORIA (*making notes as she talks*) These modern young

mothers coddle and fuss too much. She should have another child quickly—be the best thing for you both.

Bob. We can't afford any more.

Victoria. Nonsense! Only a matter of a few pounds, and a child costs little or nothing to maintain. A bit more washing, a bit more noise perhaps; and if Sally would take notice of what I say, she'd have no trouble in rearing them.

Bob. Mother, don't you think it's wrong for us to keep on living here? We're not just a married couple, we're a family.

Victoria (*turning round to stare at him*) Even so, my dear Robert, you're not disturbing anybody in the very least.

Bob. But Peter's here, and Betty, and you. Seems a bit of a crowd now we've got the youngster, and besides, it can't be much fun for Peter and Betty with a crying child in the house.

Victoria. I've heard no complaints, and what they think is of no account. If you're trying to tell me that you are dissatisfied with your home . . .

Bob (*moving* c) It's hardly that, but I thought perhaps it was about time we went off and made a home of our own, so we wouldn't bother people.

Victoria. That's very nice and thoughtful of you, Robert, but you mustn't dream of doing such a thing. I should feel hurt if I thought you wanted to leave your old home where you've lived so happily all these years.

Bob (*moving nearer to Victoria*) It isn't that I want to leave, Mother . . .

Victoria. Then you mustn't worry any more. I'm still the head of the house, and until I want to turn you out—(*she smiles*) you'll stay, even if you have half a dozen more children. We've plenty of room, fortunately, and there's no reason why we shouldn't all go on living here together. Although you've grown up, it's nice to have my boys still living with me. (*She turns back to her work again*)

Bob (*moving slowly to the armchair* rc) Thanks, Mother, but I don't think you quite understand how Sally and I feel.

Victoria (*turning to look at him*) Ah! So Sally is the restless one. She wants to break away and set up house?

Bob. Don't blame Sally, Mother; we both think the same, at least, we've discussed it together.

Victoria. I see.

(*There is a pause*)

(*She rises and moves to* r *of the table*) And I always imagined you were so happy in the old home.

Bob. We are, but after all, we're living with in-laws.

Victoria. Do you call your mother an "in-law"?

Bob. You are to Sally.

Victoria (*sitting* r *of the table*) Robert, you are disturbing me very much with this talk. May I ask how you would go about setting up house elsewhere? It costs money, you know. Living here saves you quite a lot.

BOB. I know it does. As a matter of fact, I wanted to broach the money question, Mother. (*He sits on the left arm of the armchair* RC) I wondered whether you could see your way to give me a few more pounds a week?

VICTORIA. So that you could live away from me?

BOB (*laughing a little*) A funny way of putting it.

VICTORIA. But that's what you mean, isn't it? You think you ought to break away from home, and I'm to provide extra money to do it.

BOB. Mother, we're not poor, are we? In fact, I'd guess we're jolly well off. At least, you are.

VICTORIA. We're not poor, thanks to my constant attention to the business. Eighteen years ago, when your father died, I was left with you young children and a business not very thriving. In these eighteen years, you know what has happened in the business without my going into detail.

BOB (*rising and crossing above Victoria to* L *of the table*) Yes, we're among the top ones in our own lines, thanks to you.

VICTORIA. It hasn't been easy. Luckily I had business sense and a good commercial training, and we've made good—and we've made money.

BOB. You've done a grand job, Mother. I wonder how you keep up, especially considering your age. (*He sits* L *of the table*)

VICTORIA. My age? My dear boy, I'm barely fifty. I'm as young and capable as ever I was. You young people seem to think we're decrepit at fifty.

BOB. No, not at all, but I wondered whether you felt sometimes you'd like a bit of the load taken off you. After all, Peter and I have grown up now, and we might help you more in the future, if given a chance.

VICTORIA. I don't quite see what you're driving at, Robert. I hope you're not hinting in a subtle way that I should gracefully make way for you and Peter to run the business?

BOB. Oh, I wouldn't presume to suggest that, but I only wanted you to realize that after twelve years I think I know all there is about making ropes and selling them.

VICTORIA. Thank you, Robert, for being so frank. You've certainly given me something to think about. (*She rises and moves up towards the window*)

BOB. I hope you're not cross with me, Mother. (*He rises*)

VICTORIA. No, only jolted a little. You're making me realize I'm getting older, and you're growing up.

(*The sound of the door bell is heard off*)

BOB. Well, that can't be helped, can it?

VICTORIA. Unfortunately, no.

(HETTY, *a servant in the thirties enters up* LC *and shows in a visitor,* MRS GRACE STEVENS. *She is a woman about Victoria's age, dressed fussily. She laughs a lot, talks quickly, but is a bright, harmless, pleasant woman, rather like a well-dressed barmaid*)

HETTY. Mrs Stevens is here to see you, Mrs Anson. (*She holds the door open for* GRACE *to enter*)

GRACE. Oh, hello! So you are in, Vicky? Good evening, Robert. I thought I'd pop in as I was passing, and have a minute with you.

(HETTY *exits up* LC)

BOB. Good. Mother will be glad of a change from me.

GRACE. I don't believe that. If I had a son, I wouldn't thank anybody for interrupting our little cosy chat.

VICTORIA. That's all right, Grace. We've finished our cosy chat.

BOB (*moving up to the door* LC) Excuse me, won't you, Mrs Stevens? I'd better see if Sally's managing that child.

GRACE. Ah, of course, the little one. Impossible to imagine you a granny, Vicky. What a scream!

(BOB *exits*)

VICTORIA. I don't feel a granny, and I hope I don't look it.

GRACE. You look wonderful. I don't know how you do it. You work like a slave, and I do nothing at all, and you still look no older than me.

VICTORIA. Well, I'm only a year older.

GRACE. I know, but if anything, you look a year younger. (*She crosses to the fireplace and glances at her reflection in the mirror*)

VICTORIA. Thank you. Praise from you is praise indeed.

GRACE. But you keep your figure so well, Vicky. I do envy you. How do you manage it?

VICTORIA. Work. You should try it. It would be a new experience for you. (*She moves to* L *of the sofa*)

GRACE (*laughing, and not at all upset*) You are an old tease! I say, Vicky, I'm on my way to a meeting to arrange the annual County Club Ball, for next month. Would you like to come along with me? It would be quite all right, and you'd know everybody there, and they'd be so thrilled to see you.

VICTORIA. Afraid I can't, Grace, I wanted to do some sorting out.

GRACE (*sitting at the right end of the sofa*) Oh, your business! Do you ever do anything else, or think of anything else? You really are naughty, Vicky, keeping your nose in the old works all the time. The way you go on; well, you've no right to look as you do.

You should be a white-haired old hag by this time—you deserve to be.

VICTORIA (*smiling*) Sorry to disappoint you.

GRACE. But you know what I mean. I'm not being nasty, dear, but really you are so unfair to yourself. You're working all day, and thinking probably half the night over your precious business, and what's it all for? You're pretty well off, I know . . .

VICTORIA (*sitting beside Grace*) Grace, if I don't do it, who will? You know very well that after Ernest died, I've had to carry on.

GRACE. I know that, but what's the need now? You've got into the habit of carrying on, and so you keep on carrying on. You've been doing a man's job for years. Isn't it time to think of letting the men do the man's job?

(VICTORIA *gives a start at this remark*)

Oh, sorry if I'm talking out of turn. I don't want to say anything I shouldn't.

VICTORIA. It's very odd you should say that. I've had a similar reminder a few minutes ago. (*She pauses*) Would you say my family were quite grown-up now, Grace?

GRACE. I certainly should. Why, you're a grandmother, Vicky.

VICTORIA. You needn't remind me.

GRACE. But you asked me if they were . . .

VICTORIA. Yes, I know, but I meant, are they competent grown-ups? Are my boys men now?

GRACE. Of course they are. Robert's quite the family man, isn't he? And so sensible, I always think.

VICTORIA (*thoughtfully*) Yes, I suppose he is.

(BETTY *enters up* LC. *She is a pretty girl of thirty, who could look very attractive if well-groomed. She has been kept down by her mother and accepted as a family help in the house. She is dressed rather sombrely. She moves* R *to the sofa, and smiles shyly down at Grace*)

GRACE. Hello, Betty dear, haven't seen you for ages. Are you well?

BETTY. Yes, thank you, Mrs Stevens. (*She moves down* R *to the armchair*)

VICTORIA. Have you checked that laundry, Betty, and is everything in reasonable condition?

BETTY (*pausing in her move*) Yes, Mother. This time it's all correct.

GRACE. Betty, I've been trying to persuade your mother to come with me to a meeting. She'd enjoy it if she came, but she won't. Wouldn't it do her good to get out for a change?

BETTY. Yes. Why not go, Mother? (*She sits in the armchair* R) I'll be staying in . . .

VICTORIA. Grace, I've already told you I'm busy, and besides, I've asked Father to call tonight, so please don't bother any more, either of you.

GRACE. There, Betty, we're told off. I might have known you wouldn't move out. (*She rises*) You know, some day you're going to find yourself an old woman, Vicky, and you'll be wishing you'd had a bit more fun whilst you could take it.

VICTORIA. You mean the sort of thing you do? Bridge parties, dances, motor trips and gadding about generally?

GRACE (*smiling and nodding*) Yes, it's grand fun.

BETTY (*enviously*) It must be. You do enjoy yourself, don't you, Mrs Stevens?

GRACE. You bet I do! I might be fat and fifty, but I try to get the best out of life before I get too old. It soon comes, you know. It's later than you think. Time marches on, as they say.

VICTORIA. We're not all made the same. (*She rises*)

GRACE (*moving* c) If I had your looks and figure, I wouldn't be spending every night at home. As it is, considering my handicaps, I don't do badly. Fortunately, there's plenty of fellows who still believe that saying, "The older the fiddle..." You know ... (*She gives a broad grin and a wink*)

VICTORIA. You're just as bad as ever. The same old Grace as twenty-five years ago.

GRACE. Not quite. Twenty-five years ago the men used to chase me, and now—whilst I don't exactly say I do the chasing—I will admit I meet 'em halfway!

(BETTY *and* VICTORIA *laugh*)

It hasn't perhaps the same thrill, but if you want a bit of company, you've got to do it, haven't you? Men are proper devils, most of 'em, but they are good company after all. What do you say, Betty?

VICTORIA. Betty knows nothing of men in the way you mean, and isn't in the least interested.

GRACE (*with a queer look at Betty*) Oh, isn't she? I can hardly believe that. Maybe she lacks opportunity. (*She gives Victoria a steady look*)

VICTORIA. Betty is a sensible girl. She's far happier living quietly at home than gadding about, aren't you, dear?

BETTY (*embarrassed*) I suppose so. I don't really know.

GRACE (*about to leave*) Well, this won't get me to that meeting, so I'd better move. Vicky, if you won't come along now, promise you'll come to the Ball next month? You've been a member for years and never come to anything. We'll have a fine time, do you good. What about it?

VICTORIA. I'll see, nearer the time.

GRACE (*moving up* LC *to the door*) That means you won't come. Well, I'll remind you, anyway. So long, Betty. Good-bye, Vicky.

(GRACE *waves her hand and exits, humming "Enjoy yourself, it's later than you think"* VICTORIA *crosses down* L *to the desk, sits, and resumes her perusal of the papers.* BETTY *rises and stands by the fire, clearly thinking of the breezy Grace and what she has said*)

BETTY (*staring at the door up* LC) Doesn't she just ooze vitality and, as the French say—*bonhomie?*

VICTORIA (*abstracted*) What? Oh, Grace, you mean? Yes, she's a lively one, but hardly an example to copy.

BETTY (*moving to the armchair* RC) She must have been very attractive when she was younger.

VICTORIA. She was, and never short of a man. She had two husbands before she was thirty.

BETTY (*staring into space*) I shall be thirty this summer.

VICTORIA (*looking up*) Good gracious, so you will! How startling; to think of my Betty thirty! You children seem determined tonight to remind me that I'm getting on.

BETTY (*quickly*) Why, has Bob been talking to you?

VICTORIA. Yes, and he's disturbed me a little.

BETTY. Bob's been getting very restless lately, Mother. (*She sits in the armchair up* RC)

VICTORIA. You mean *Sally.*

BETTY. No, not just Sally. They're both of the same mind.

VICTORIA. So I gathered. I expect you know more than I do.

BETTY. About what?

VICTORIA. His extraordinary notion of leaving here and setting up a home of his own.

BETTY. Well, I'm not altogether surprised.

VICTORIA (*rising impatiently and moving* C) But what's wrong with this? (*She indicates the comfortable room with a gesture*) Nothing could be nicer for them or more comfortable. Don't you agree?

BETTY (*quietly and without enthusiasm*) Yes, Mother.

VICTORIA. I've always tried to do the right thing for all of you, and when my son tells me he wants to break away, I don't understand it at all.

BETTY (*quietly*) I didn't think you would.

VICTORIA. Why, do you?

BETTY. Yes, it's quite natural they should want to. They're a family, another generation.

VICTORIA (*surprised*) That's what Bob said. But that isn't all. He hinted that I ought to consider allowing him much more control in the business, and Peter as well. My goodness, I might be a decrepit old woman of eighty instead of a woman in the prime of life!

BETTY. Mother, he wouldn't mean it unkindly. Bob and Peter are no longer boys, but experienced busines-men, and jolly clever, too. Everybody else knows that.

B

VICTORIA. And *I* don't, I suppose you mean? (*She sits in the chair* R *of the table*)

BETTY. You see them through a mother's eyes, as youngsters who still have to be managed at home and in the office.

VICTORIA. So *you're* on their side?

BETTY. I'm on nobody's side, but I can see their point.

VICTORIA. I'm afraid you're right, Betty. I still see them through a mother's eyes.

BETTY. We're lucky they haven't gone off and worked for another firm.

VICTORIA (*rising; angrily*) What a monstrous idea; they wouldn't dare. They both know perfectly well that in time the firm will be theirs.

BETTY. It may be a long time, Mother. Meanwhile they have to live, and they're ambitious.

VICTORIA. They both have a decent living wage, they should be satisfied.

BETTY. It depends on what you want. What hope has Peter of getting married, poor boy?

VICTORIA. I hope Peter has no such nonsense in his head.

BETTY. Is it nonsense? He's twenty-six.

VICTORIA. And, I suppose, he wants to marry that nitwit of a girl Pauline? (*She moves down to the desk*)

BETTY. He does. They're very much in love. (*She sighs*) It must be nice for Pauline, or any other girl, having a man doting on her.

VICTORIA. You sound almost envious.

BETTY. Yes, I am, if you must know. Suppose I told you I wanted to marry?

VICTORIA (*smiling*) What, you?

BETTY. The idea seems amusing to you, Mother.

VICTORIA (*sitting at the desk*) Betty dear, forgive my smiling, but I never think of you in that way—marrying, or bothering with men . . .

BETTY (*rising and moving* C) No, you wouldn't. Ever since I was seventeen I've been the housekeeper, haven't I? I've had about thirteen years looking after younger brothers and the house.

VICTORIA. And how very well you've done it. You have that satisfaction, and I know the boys are most grateful for what you do, just as I am.

BETTY. Thank you. But thirteen years is a long time, Mother.

VICTORIA. But you've not been unhappy. You've had a lovely home, you've not had to go out and mix in the world with a lot of unpleasant people. You've been spared a great deal, if you knew it, my dear. It isn't like you to complain.

BETTY (*moving to Victoria*) Because I've never said much, you've all imagined I was happy. You've taken it for granted that I was. In a way I have been happy, Mother, but I've been aware I was missing something, and more especially lately. When I see

Bob with Sally and Peter with Pauline, I know what I've missed.

VICTORIA. I'm surprised to hear this from you.

BETTY. Why should you be? I'm perfectly normal, I think I'm passably decent-looking, I can enjoy myself—given the chance. You might say I'm just the average woman, no more or less, so I see no need for surprise.

VICTORIA. When you put it like that, perhaps I shouldn't be surprised. I hope you're not suggesting I've stood in your way, Betty? Are you blaming me?

BETTY (*turning away from Victoria*) Oh, what's the use of talking of blame? Let's call it simply "circumstances", and leave it at that.

VICTORIA (*rising; angrily*) I won't let it go at that. Now you've said so much, tell me more. Really, you're all upsetting me tonight. I'm getting shocks I don't like.

BETTY. No need to be angry, Mother. I'm only letting off steam.

VICTORIA. Yes, but you meant what you said. (*She calms down a little*) I want you to know how completely ignorant I've been about it all. I'd no idea . . .

BETTY (*rather annoyed*) Oh, let's forget it. (*She crosses R to the fireplace*)

VICTORIA (*following Betty*) I'll tell you what I'll do. I'll make you a little present, and it will be a generous one. There, how will that do? (*Soothingly*) And always remember you'll be quite a wealthy girl one day.

BETTY. My idea of wealth may be different from yours, Mother.

VICTORIA. And what is yours, may I ask?

BETTY. Shall I tell you? It's having a little home of my own, with a nice man for a husband, and perhaps a child or two about the place, and doing my own housework, and shopping, and sometimes being hard-up, and sometimes having a spree when we have a few pounds to spare. That's wealth, to me.

VICTORIA. Fancy you having such thoughts, and none of us ever knew! How long have you had these ideas?

BETTY. Oh, quite a time now. For about the last ten years, I think.

VICTORIA. This is dreadfully upsetting. What can I say? (*She moves to L of the table and sits*)

BETTY. Nothing, Mother. I'm sorry I started all this.

VICTORIA. But you make me feel responsible. Perhaps I should have known long ago, but I've been so concerned with other things, and . . .

BETTY. Yes, you've been so busy.

VICTORIA (*seizing on this*) Yes, dear, I have been busy. Somebody had to be busy when your father died. I had to step into his shoes. I had to manage the business and the home.

Betty (*moving* c) I know, Mother. Please don't think I'm blaming you. I'm not. I'm only confessing. It would be better to drop the subject altogether. I don't know why we started it.

Victoria. I'm glad. At least I've learned something about my own daughter.

(William Fitzmarren, *Victoria's father, enters up* lc. *He is a wiry old fellow of seventy-eight, but he looks about sixty-five. He is an Irishman, and the usual cheery, likeable type, retaining his Irish brogue. He is as usual full of hearty good humour*)

William. So this is where you are, my dear. Hullo, Elizabeth! It's grand to see your pretty face again. But you're lookin' a bit worried. Can't have that. Pretty girls shouldn't be worried. (*He comes down* c, *taking his pipe from his pocket*)

Victoria. Father, what's brought you round? We don't often have this pleasure.

William. What a woman! (*To Betty*) She's askin' a daft question, and she's the one who sent for me. Wasn't it yourself who asked me to attend for a few brief words, and here I am to obey your royal commands, to be sure.

Victoria. Oh, of course I did. So much has been happening, I'd forgotten for the moment.

William. Well now, as I'm here, what's your news? For something of importance it must be to send for your old Dad. (*He looks at his watch*) And I hope you won't be long, as I'm due to meet a fella in—the near future.

Victoria. At the *Rose and Crown*, or the *Miller's Arms?*

William. What should I be wantin' in such places, now?

Victoria. I could guess if I liked. (*She rises and moves* l *to the desk*) Betty, I think perhaps I'd better see Grandy alone. A bit of family business.

William. And what harm will the lass be doin' if she stays? (*To Betty*) Come, my girl, let's settle down and hear what your mother has to say. (*He moves to the armchair* rc)

Victoria. If you don't mind, Father, Betty can find something else more useful to do.

William (*pausing; to Betty*) There, you're dismissed from the royal presence. It bodes ill for me if I'm to be left alone with your mother.

Betty (*kissing him*) So long, Grandy. I may see you as you go.

William. If I'm not carried out on a stretcher.

(Betty *exits up* lc)

She's a nice girl—not a bit like you either; make a fine wife, should have married years ago. I wonder why she hasn't. (*He sits in the armchair* rc) Funny thing how some of these women ugly as a Dublin tramcar can find a man, and others, like her, can't manage it.

VICTORIA. We won't go into that at the moment. (*She sits at the desk and turns over the papers*)

WILLIAM. What will we be goin' into, then? From the look on your bonny face, it's somethin' serious.

VICTORIA. Father, when I made you a fixed monthly allowance, I considered I was being generous.

WILLIAM. So you were, my dear. Didn't I say at the time, "There's a lovely daughter for any man to be proud of, and one who appreciates her old dad at his true worth"?

VICTORIA. Good. Glad you admit it. (*She picks up some bills from the desk*) So if I make a mild protest about these I shan't be unreasonable. (*She rises and moves towards him*)

WILLIAM (*rising*) What in Heaven's name have you got there? A nasty-lookin' bundle of papers.

VICTORIA. They are. They're bills—your bills. Sent to me because you've dodged payment.

WILLIAM. Now what can these be for? I'm not in the habit of runnin' up bills.

VICTORIA. If you don't know, I can easily remind you. (*She sits in the chair R of the table*) One here for taxis, journeys to Epsom, Aintree, Doncaster, York, and even to Newmarket.

WILLIAM. Yes, I remember. I've been doin' a bit of business in those parts. (*He sits in the armchair*)

VICTORIA. Did it pay?

WILLIAM. To tell you the truth, I was a little bit out of pocket. Ah, the frailty of man and beast at a time of crisis!

VICTORIA. Another one for spirits and tobacco—almost thirty pounds.

WILLIAM. Wicked, the price of things today. It costs an awful lot for a man to get himself into a cheerful mood.

VICTORIA. I have some more here one for an overcoat—another for an umbrella—another for a new hat. A bill here from a florist . . . (*She turns over the handul of papers, and looks steadily at William*)

(*There is a short pause*)

WILLIAM. Ah, stop your morbid recital, woman! I've heard enough. Is this what you've brought me down to hear? If so, you've got a strange notion of entertainment and hospitality. (*He rises and retreats towards the fireplace*) Worrying an old man of my age about a few paltry bills sent by soulless tradesmen!

VICTORIA (*rising, moving to the desk and replacing the papers*) I only wanted to tell you, Father, this has got to stop. I'll pay these bills this time, but from now on you'll live on that allowance.

WILLIAM. But, Vicky, my dear, think of the cost of living. It fair depresses a man. I wonder I have the heart to go out of doors at all. A pound note goes nowhere. Just about half a bottle of whisky—that's the rate of exchange nowadays!

VICTORIA. How you spend your allowance is nothing to me, but beyond the allowance I will not go. (*She moves* C) You'll have to limit yourself.

WILLIAM. Fancy askin' an Irishman to limit himself! You're disappointin' me, Vicky my darlin'. I never thought the day would come when you'd be sittin' in judgement on your old father. What about a little of the milk of human kindness? (*He sits on the right arm of the sofa*)

VICTORIA. Never mind milk of human kindness, you old rascal! I'm treating you well, and you know it. I'm doing this for your own good.

WILLIAM. Isn't that the most irritating phrase—"for your own good"? I used to hear it as a boy seventy years ago, and it's still being used against me. Even your own dear mother used to say it to me.

VICTORIA. I'll bet she did. Mother must have had a rare old time dealing with you.

WILLIAM. Ah, your mother was a fine woman—one in a thousand, even if she wasn't Irish. I do believe now, Vicky, in many ways you resemble your mother.

VICTORIA. I'm sure I'm not like you, and a good job, too! If I'd been as feckless as you, I don't know what would have become of us all.

WILLIAM. Ah, you've got your mother's good sense—she was a Lancashire girl—and you've got your father's good looks. You know the Fitzmarrens were all good-lookers. Good old Irish stock we are. Some day I must dig up their history.

VICTORIA. I shouldn't risk it. You might dig up something better left alone.

WILLIAM. I believe one of the old family was a pal of George the Fourth.

VICTORIA. H'm, that's just what I mean. (*She gives him a quizzical look*)

WILLIAM (*rising and moving* L) I was just ponderin' over what you've been tellin' me, Vicky. About spendin' and the like. It costs a lot of money to keep alive nowadays. Indeed, I'd be cheaper dead. Were you by any chance intendin' me to take you serious like?

VICTORIA. Decidedly. What do you think I've been talking for? (*She sits in the armchair* RC)

WILLIAM (*sighing*) Ah well, I've not many more years left in me, and I would like to go out with pleasant thoughts of my own dear generous daughter. (*He sits in the chair* L *of the table*)

VICTORIA. You can stop that talk. I know it too well. You're not likely to pop off yet. You'll live to be a hundred, so I've a good many years yet to support you. How old are you, Father?

WILLIAM. I'm seventy-eight.

VICTORIA. And you'd pass for sixty-five.

WILLIAM. That's with looking after myself and livin' a good life.

VICTORIA. Well, I'll admit that it's with looking after yourself.

WILLIAM. I've never been a worrier. It's worry that kills.

VICTORIA. How very true. You've always let other people worry. Mother worried for you, and I've done it since. I often wonder what would have happened to you if we hadn't cared for you.

WILLIAM. Begad, that's a sobering thought! And mention of the word makes me ask if you happen to have such a thing about the house as a drop o' liquor?

VICTORIA. You know quite well I don't have drinks in this house.

WILLIAM. Aye, I know that's been your rule, but I thought maybe you'd reformed, and . . . Ah, well, you'll compel me to make a call on the way home, much against my inclination, but for the sake of my health. (*He rises and moves* C)

VICTORIA. I hope you're taking notice of what I've said, Father.

WILLIAM (*moving a few steps towards the door up* L C) I'll be turnin' it over all the night through. I won't sleep a wink. (*He turns to face her*) Vicky, whilst you were blatherin' away to me, I was thinkin' you're gettin' into a hard woman.

VICTORIA. Not hard, I hope, only business-like. I've had to be a business woman for a long time now.

WILLIAM. I know all that, and well you've done, God knows. But must you keep going on and driving yourself so hard? To my mind you should think now of going easier. You've got two fine boys—let them do the work.

VICTORIA. It's very odd you should start on this topic tonight. (*She rises*) There seems to be a conspiracy in the house. Are you in it, too?

WILLIAM. A conspiracy? God forbid. (*He moves down to sit in the chair* R *of the table*) I'm one of the few Irishmen of character who's never been in a conspiracy.

VICTORIA. So you think I should retire?

WILLIAM. Now, I didn't say anythin' so drastic, but take it easier. If you dropped dead, the place would go on somehow. How old are you? Fifty?

VICTORIA. Forty-nine. (*She sits in the armchair* R C)

WILLIAM. You hardly look it. As Gilbert says, "You'd pass very well for forty-three in the dusk with the light behind you." (*He pauses*) And you're still good-lookin'. What you want is a man.

VICTORIA (*giving him a look*) What!

WILLIAM. Soften you down, give you a new interest.

VICTORIA. Do you mean I should marry again?

WILLIAM. What else would I be meanin'?

VICTORIA. But I've a grown-up family.

WILLIAM. All the more reason for doin' it. Leave your family to themselves. You've been like an old hen cluckin' away with her chicks around her for years.

VICTORIA (*doubtfully*) I'm too old—at least, I think I am. Do you think so, Father?

WILLIAM. Nothing of the kind. Why, I might as well confess that if I could find a nice little woman with a bit of money who'd be willing to take me on, I'd be after her like a shot. I wouldn't have a young one—take too much watching. I'd want one I could leave safe at home while I went out.

VICTORIA. Father, what will you say next? (*She rises and moves* R *to the fireplace*) Don't you think you'd better be off, and make your call, before you say anything worse?

WILLIAM. Just what was in my mind. My throat's as dry as the desert sand. (*He rises and moves up* LC)

VICTORIA (*turning to look at him*) Father, whatever put that extraordinary idea into your head that I should think of marrying again?

WILLIAM (*moving down a few steps*) It's hard to say exactly. Inspiration comes to me, you might call it. I've been weighing you up, and I thought what a shame that such a grand woman should be wastin' her life, poring over figures and books, and doin' a man's job, instead of which she could be delightin' the heart of a fine fella, for there must be many a man who'd like to come and lay his heart at your feet.

VICTORIA (*impressed*) I wonder? How strange, everybody's making me think madly tonight.

WILLIAM. Now, you're goin' to heed my words, I hope. Get something more out of life before it's too late. (*He turns and moves up to the door* LC) Well, I'll be off. Oh, Vicky, a last word. (*He turns at the door*) I think it 'ud be best if we agreed no more bills, no more debts of mine to settle, but instead, you increase the allowance a trifle. Not so much as you'd hardly notice it, but just enough for me to have the real comforts of life. Eh?

VICTORIA (*smiling*) All right, you old rogue. We'll see about it.

WILLIAM. You're my own darlin' daughter. Good night and God bless ye!

WILLIAM *exits up* LC. VICTORIA *smiles as he goes, and then stands looking thoughtfully into the fire as—*

the CURTAIN *falls*

ACT II

SCENE—*The same. About a month later. One evening, eight o'clock.*
The room seems brighter. There is a set of new, coloured curtains at
the window, drawn close, and large vases of flowers are placed about the
room. There are new, bright cushions on the sofa and the chairs.

When the CURTAIN *rises* BETTY *is sitting in the armchair down* R,
manicuring her nails. She is now quite smartly dressed, wearing high-
heeled shoes and nylon stockings, and her hair is attractively done. HETTY
the maid, enters up LC, *carrying a tray with glasses, a decanter of*
whisky and a syphon. She places the tray on the table LC.

BETTY. What's that, Hetty?

HETTY. Something I was told to bring in here and leave. I
think it's whisky.

BETTY. What? Who told you to bring it in, and where's it come
from?

HETTY (*moving* C) Your mother's orders, Miss Betty. I don't
know any more. But if I might say so, I never thought I'd see
strong drink in this house, but we live and learn.

BETTY. It's very odd.

HETTY. I'll say it is, and not the only thing either.

BETTY. You've noticed things, have you, Hetty?

HETTY. Well, I'd be a bit slow if I hadn't. I'll tell you one
thing, and I hope you'll not think me cheeky. Your mother's a
different woman these last few weeks. She doesn't argue with me
half as much. She lets me do my own.

BETTY. Must be getting absent-minded.

HETTY. I don't care what it is, so long as she keeps on in the
same frame of mind. Reminds me when I was young. My father
used to come home drunk regular, and I used to tell me mother
she should try and stop him, but she said it was the only time he
was ever kind and good-tempered, so why bother? (*She looks round
the room*) Looks nice in here now. Them new curtains brighten
things up.

BETTY. We're going to have some in the dining-room, and a
new carpet as well.

HETTY. Not before they're needed. Let the good work go on.
(*She turns to Betty*) While you're at it, Miss Betty, you might get me
a new vacuum.

BETTY. All right, I'll see to it.

HETTY (*surprised*) Will you reely? I'll go and see if I can think of anythin' else while the goin's good.

(*The front-door bell is heard off*)

BETTY. That will be Mrs Stevens, calling for Mother.

(HETTY *goes out up* LC. *After a few seconds she returns and shows in* GRACE, *who is very daringly dressed, looking rather like a publican's wife out for the evening in her low-cut, bright evening gown. She sails in, large and florid, holding her long gloves and wearing a loose, roomy fur coat*)

GRACE (*coming down* C) Hello, Betty! Mother not down yet? (*She takes off her coat and lays it over the armchair* RC)

(HETTY *exits up* LC)

BETTY. No. Won't you sit down, Mrs Stevens?

GRACE. Thanks, but it's not so easy sittin' down, trussed up as I am!

BETTY. You look very smart.

GRACE (*moving* R *and looking in the mirror over the mantelpiece*) It's taken me hours to tog myself up. I should look a world-beater, but I know I don't! What can you do with a figure like mine? My dress-maker's very polite, but I'll bet she thinks a lot. I must be a proper headache to her.

BETTY. She's done very well.

GRACE (*moving to the armchair* RC, *then pausing*) No, if I get down, I'll not get up so easy, and my corsets might not stand the strain. (*She moves to the chair* R *of the table and sits on the edge of it*) I'll play for safety. (*She looks at Betty*) You're looking pretty to-night, Betty.

BETTY. Must be the new frock. (*She rises and displays the frock*)

GRACE. It looks nice, but then you can look nice in anything. Your hair's so natural and your figure's so slim. Eeeh, you're lucky! But then you can't have it every way. I will eat what I like, and I like the wrong things, so I pay for it. (*She laughs loudly*)

BETTY. Never mind, you enjoy yourself and you're healthy.

GRACE. Touch wood, I am. (*She touches the edge of the chair*) And I enjoy myself. I'm goin' to have a good time tonight. Always do, you know.

BETTY. It's rather special tonight, I suppose? (*She moves to* R *of the armchair* RC *and sits on the arm*)

GRACE. It's the event of the season, the classy affair. All those who matter and them who think they matter will be there. It's a bit frosty at first, everybody prim and proper, but we thaw them out after an hour, and it ends up like a Christmas party.

BETTY. Nobody could be serious for long if you were about.

GRACE. So they tell me. They leave it to me to get things moving. Eeeh, but I'm glad your mother's comin'! I never expected she would. When she rang me up the other day, I nearly had a heart attack. Said she was lookin' forward to it. Imagine Vicky, she who never goes anywhere!

BETTY. Mother's somewhat changed lately.

GRACE. She must have, according to what I've heard. Takin' on a new lease of life, is what they say. I hear she's gaddin' about a bit.

BETTY. Well, she's not staying at home so much.

GRACE. Showin' herself more generous, too, isn't she?

BETTY. I think she is.

GRACE. You know very well she is. She's decked you out with some decent clothes at last.

BETTY (*pretending to be shocked*) Mrs Stevens!

GRACE. Oh, I can say what I like. I'm your mother's eldest pal. I'd say the same to her face, so you needn't worry.

BETTY. I think poor Mother realizes she's been doing too much, so she's going to ease off a bit.

GRACE. You've said it! And like most folk in a similar way, she'll go too strong if she's not careful.

BETTY. How do you mean?

GRACE. I've heard a few rumours, Betty. News soon spreads in this town. She's very pally with that new chap who's come here lately, that fellow with the electric works.

BETTY. Oh, you mean Harry Bateman? (*She rises and stands facing down stage*)

GRACE. That's him. Why, do you know him?

BETTY (*crossing above Grace to L. of the table*) Yes, I've met him. He's rather nice, too.

GRACE. She's been about with him in his car and at the theatre.

BETTY. I believe she is friendly with him. But what of it? (*She leans over the back of the chair L of the table*)

GRACE. Well, you never know, especially with one like Vicky, who's not gone about for years. I know what men are. They're cute, up to all sorts of tricks, and when they see a bit o' money . . . (*She rises and moves C*) Oh well, it's her business, and good luck to her, I say. Your mother's got her head screwed on. She should know what she's doin', but we can all be a bit soft when a plausible man comes along, otherwise they'd have a job to fill the *News of the World* every Sunday.

BETTY (*laughing*) You are terrible, really! (*She sits L of the table*)

GRACE. Don't take any notice of me. I *will* have my joke.

BETTY. Tell me, what are people saying about Mother?

GRACE. They're just wondering what she's up to, and so am I. (*She moves to the mirror over the fireplace and looks at herself*) When a widow of fifty suddenly starts blossomin' out, dressin' herself up, spendin' money regardless, then it looks as if she's on the warpath.

BETTY. For what?

GRACE. Never mind. (*She turns away from the mirror*) We'll see. Time will tell, as they say. If she gets set on a certain idea, she'll take some stoppin'. I wonder how long she'll be. She must be makin' a good job of herself all this time.

BETTY. It's the new dress, I expect, but she wouldn't let me help, so I left her to it.

(VICTORIA *enters up* LC, *looking extremely attractive in black, which makes her appear slimmer than ever. Her hair is smart, and her small amount of jewellery makes an ensemble of good taste. She looks about forty*)

GRACE (*moving to Victoria*) Oh hullo, Vicky! At last you're ready. My, you are a fair treat to look at! I shall look like one of the Ugly Sisters at the pantomime! No hope for me tonight, Betty, with you mother around!

VICTORIA (*coming down* C) Do I look passable? How's the length, Betty?

BETTY (*rising*) Perfect, Mother. You do look nice. People would take you for my elder sister.

VICTORIA (*moving to the mirror over the fireplace*) I hope my back hasn't any spots on it. I haven't exposed it for years to the public gaze.

GRACE. I don't chance *my* back. (*She turns so that her back is to the audience*) I let the front go as much as I dare! (*She turns round again to face the audience*)

VICTORIA. I didn't know whether you would be calling, Grace. (*She smoothes her already tidy hair, looking in the mirror*)

GRACE. But I thought you understood I'd call, and we'd get a taxi from here?

VICTORIA. Oh, I wasn't quite sure. Harry Bateman said he'd call for me, so we'll be all right.

GRACE (*winking at Betty*) Oh, I see. Harry Bateman's picking you up. Will he mind my coming?

VICTORIA. Of course not. How silly of you.

GRACE. I don't know him very well, but you do, don't you, Vicky?

VICTORIA. We've met a few times, various places, recently.

GRACE. Nice, isn't he?

VICTORIA. Very nice indeed. Isn't he, Betty?

(BETTY *makes no reply*)

Betty likes him, so he must be nice. Oh, Betty, I wish you'd warn Hetty that Mr Bateman will be calling for us, and would you mind getting my fur coat and gloves? I've left them ready in my room.

BETTY. Yes, Mother.

(BETTY *moves up* LC *above the table and exits*)

GRACE. I never expected you'd come to this Ball.

VICTORIA. But I told you last week I should.

GRACE. I thought you were kidding me, and yet I ought to have believed you, for nobody can tell what you'll do next! This last few weeks you've become a different woman, Vicky.

VICTORIA. And do you like the different woman, Grace?

GRACE. Lookin' at you now, I can hardly credit it is you. (*She sits on the left arm of the sofa*) You look younger, smarter and so changed—I can't describe it exactly.

VICTORIA. No, I shouldn't try. I'm having a fresh look at the great world outside my home and the office. Isn't it time after eighteen years?

GRACE. Yes, but I'm wonderin' what's behind all this?

VICTORIA. Oh, you think I'm planning something? As a matter of fact, I am. I've decided I'll get married again.

GRACE (*rising quickly*) Married again? My goodness! You've kept it dark. Who is it, Vicky?

VICTORIA. I don't know.

GRACE. Come on, tell me. I'm your oldest pal. I won't split on you!

VICTORIA (*moving to Grace*) I tell you, I don't know. I've only decided I'll marry again. Whom I shall marry is another matter.

GRACE. So you've decided, just like that, eh? (*She moves a little away from Victoria and turns to look at her in surprise*) It takes me breath away to hear you say it so cool, like saying, "I'm going to buy a new hat tomorrow."

VICTORIA (*sitting on the right arm of the armchair* RC) Isn't the first thing to decide whether you want a thing or not? If I didn't know I wanted to marry again, I shouldn't know what to say if somebody asked me, should I?

GRACE. Well, of all the sauce! I might tell you I've been wantin' to marry again for years, but I wouldn't dare say I've decided to marry again. How do you know you can?

VICTORIA. I don't—yet.

GRACE. But you must have somebody in mind.

VICTORIA. Not necessarily. It's merely a general idea.

GRACE. What started the idea? (*She moves to Victoria*)

VICTORIA. Oh, several things. Bob spoke to me recently about the works; you told me I should get out of my shell, and perhaps it was Father who really made me think of making a change.

GRACE. He would, the old villain. He very nearly proposed to me one night when he'd had a few.

VICTORIA. How awful!

GRACE (*moving away a little*) I didn't mind. It was nice to know somebody thought so much of me. He's very young for his age, you know.

(*There is a slight pause*)

(*She nudges Victoria in curiosity*) I say, Vicky, is it Harry Bateman?

VICTORIA. It might be. He is taking rather an interest in me.

GRACE. Take the advice of one who's been trying for years. If he's like that and you like him, go all out. I never get fellas that are keen on me. They think I'm a grand bit o' fun, we have a good time together, but that's all there is to it. It's sickenin'.

VICTORIA. I'm not rushing into anything until I'm sure, but I do like Harry.

GRACE. So if he pops the question, you'll clinch it?

VICTORIA. Perhaps.

(BETTY *enters up* LC, *carrying Victoria's coat and gloves*)

BETTY. Here's your coat, Mother, and gloves. (*She lays the coat over the back of the sofa, and the gloves on top of it*)

VICTORIA (*rising*) Thank you, dear. Now I think we're ready.

(*The sound of the doorbell is heard off*)

Ah, here he is, just at the right moment.

GRACE (*picking up her coat*) What a man! He comes just when he should. Harry knows a thing or two.

(HETTY *enters up* LC *and ushers in* HARRY BATEMAN. *Harry is a well-built, pleasant fellow, aged about forty-four. He is dressed in full evening kit, and carries a tiny bunch of flowers. His manner is quietly confident.*

HETTY *exits up* LC)

VICTORIA. Good evening, Harry. You know Grace Stevens, don't you? (*She gestures in Grace's direction*)

HARRY. How do you do, Mrs Stevens? (*He shakes hands with Grace*)

VICTORIA. And you know my daughter, Betty, of course.

HARRY (*smiling at Betty*) Oh yes, we had quite a nice time at the Rotary affair last week, hadn't we, Miss Anson?

BETTY. I enjoyed it very much. My first dance for years. (*She moves down* R *to the armchair*)

HARRY. I shouldn't have thought so. You seemed quite at home.

GRACE. So our Betty's coming out again, is she? Like Mother.

VICTORIA. Why not? The poor child hasn't had much fun lately.

HARRY (*holding out the flowers to Victoria*) Vicky, for you.

VICTORIA. Oh thanks, Harry. How lovely. I'll wear them with this frock. By the way, do you like it?

HARRY. You look wonderful. It's incredible to think you have a daughter like Betty.

BETTY (*amused*) Thank you. (*She sits in the armchair*)

HARRY. Oh, I'm sorry. I mean, Vicky looks younger than she is . . .

VICTORIA. But you don't know my age?

HARRY. No, of course not, but I mean—er . . .

GRACE. You'd better shut up, my lad. If we're all ready, I propose we ought to be making a move. There's a bit of supper first, and I'm anxious to have my money's worth before the greedy ones eat it all. You know what they are! I hope you won't mind me coming with you, Mr Bateman?

HARRY. A pleasure to accompany two charming ladies, I assure you. My car awaits you.

(*The sound of the doorbell is heard off*)

VICTORIA. That's the doorbell. We'd better move. I don't want visitors at the moment.

(HARRY *takes Victoria's coat from the sofa and helps her on with it.*
HETTY *enters up* LC *and shows in* JOHN YARDLEY. *He is a fine-looking man of sixty, easy-going and good-tempered; the family solicitor and a great friend. He is in evening dress and carries a large bunch of flowers.*
HETTY *exits up* LC)

JOHN (*greeting Victoria*) Ha! Just in time to catch you, Victoria. I wondered if I'd be too late. Good evening, Grace. Hello, Bateman, are you going to this affair, too?

HARRY. You bet. I wouldn't miss it for anything, I'm told it's *the event, so I* must show up.

JOHN. Yes, you're getting yourself in at all the local shows. For a newcomer you've not been slow.

GRACE. Hear, hear, John.

HARRY. Good for business.

VICTORIA. Harry believes in mixing business with pleasure, on occasions.

JOHN. So I've noticed. I like doing that myself. That's why I make a trip sometimes to see Victoria on business. It makes business a pleasure. (*He bows to Victoria*)

VICTORIA. John, don't tease. Harry, I suppose you know John's our family solicitor.

HARRY. A privileged position; advisor and friend as well.

JOHN. A very dear old friend, I may tell you.

GRACE (*moving a little nearer to John*) He's a good sort, but I wish you weren't a solicitor, John. Every time I look at you, I shudder, 'cos I think of wills and deeds and awful documents.

JOHN. A nice thing to say to me, isn't it, Betty? By the way, aren't you coming tonight?

BETTY. No, I'm the little Cinderella this time. I had my turn last week. I don't mind a bit. This affair will be rather elderly, I'm afraid.

HARRY. Elderly?

JOHN. That's shaken you, Bateman; see what the younger generation thinks of anybody over forty.

BETTY. Oh, I didn't mean *everybody* would be elderly.

GRACE. Come on, before she says any more. There's one grandmother here, and with a bit o' luck I should have been another.

(VICTORIA *gives Grace an angry look*)

How are we goin'? I suppose you've got a car, John?

JOHN. Yes, my man's waiting. We can all get in it.

HARRY. I've got mine. You see, I was calling for Vicky in any case . . .

GRACE (*taking John's arm*) Come on, John. You'll have to make do with me. Let them go on their own.

JOHN (*displeased*) Oh, very well.

(GRACE *leads* JOHN *firmly towards the door* LC)

Victoria, I'll leave those flowers for you. (*He escapes from Grace, places the flowers on the table and reluctantly joins her again*)

VICTORIA. Thank you, John. Are you ready, Harry?

BETTY (*rising*) Have a good time. (*She catches* HARRY'S *eye and smiles*)

HARRY. Righto. Good-bye, Cinderella.

GRACE. Good-bye. Exit the Ugly Sister.

(*They exit up* LC; JOHN *leading* GRACE, *followed by* HARRY *and* VICTORIA. *They leave the door open and the sound of their voices is heard, followed by the sound of cars driving away.*

SALLY *enters up* LC *quickly*)

SALLY. Have they just gone? I wanted to see your mother. Did she look very glamorous?

BETTY (*with feeling*) She looked wonderful. I wish I could be sure I'll look as good as that at fifty! Don't you, Sally?

(*Faint baby cries are heard off*)

SALLY (*throwing herself full length on the sofa*) If that awful child of mine doesn't behave better, I'll never see fifty. If only I had my own home, I could cope with him, but it's like crying for the moon.

(BOB *enters up* LC, *looking worried and untidy*)

BOB. He's crying a bit, but let him! I've done my best. I've pulled faces for him, jumped about like a dog, made all sorts of queer noises, but he *is not* amused, and so he can jolly well cry himself to sleep. I never knew kids could be such trouble, or else we're unlucky. I'm sure I was never such an infernal nuisance. (*He sprawls on the armchair* RC, *with his legs spreadeagled*)

BETTY. Mother says you were extremely difficult, but she didn't take any notice.

BOB. There you are, Sally, no fussing. That accounts for my good temper.

SALLY. You've got your mother's temper and temperament. (*She pauses, then sits up*) Bob, I just missed seeing her go. Betty says she looked terrific.

BOB. I don't doubt it. Mother can knock you girls right out of the picture when she really tries.

SALLY. For her age she's pretty good.

BOB. Never mind "for her age". I'm telling you that if Mother set about it, she'd give you two a run in the glamour line.

BETTY (*quietly*) I rather suspect she is setting about it, Bob.

BOB. Where's old Grandpa? I told him to call about eight to talk this business over.

SALLY. What business?

BOB. Why, Mother, of course. I want the old man's view and advice if he has any.

SALLY. What use can he be?

BOB. Well, it's his daughter; he knew Mother before we did.

BETTY. I fail to see what there is to discuss. (*She sits in the arm-chair down* R)

BOB. You don't realize what's brewing, my girl.

BETTY. Why have a family conference simply because Mother's putting on a party frock again?

BOB. If it were only that.

(*The sound of the doorbell is heard off*)

Ah, that's the old man.

SALLY. A waste of time talking to Grandpa. (*She rises and moves up towards the door* I.C)

BOB. We can at least get an opinion from him for what it's worth.

(WILLIAM FITZMARREN *enters up* LC, *looking cheery and carefree as usual. He comes down towards them.* SALLY *stands above the table so that* WILLIAM *does not see the whisky as he enters*)

BOB (*rising*) Glad you've come, Grandy. Hope it wasn't inconvenient?

WILLIAM. Well, I'm able to give you a few minutes of my valuable time before I go to a business appointment. I said to myself, "I mustn't disappoint my favourite grandson if he's wantin' the advice of his sagacious old grandfather." What's the three of you doin' here? Is this an argument? If so, I'm glad I'm invited, for I love an argument. It's the breath of life to an Irishman.

(SALLY *moves down* L)

BOB. It's a discussion.

WILLIAM. Ah well, we can soon turn it into an argument. Now if you're wantin' me to take the chair, you'd better let me have

C

the comfortable one, Robert. Away you get. (*He pushes* Bob *away from the armchair* RC *and sits down*)

(Bob *moves* L *so that he is hiding the whisky from William*)

That's better. Let me get my pipe goin', to help my thoughts. Elizabeth, my dear, you're lookin' as pretty as your mother used to look twenty years ago. And talkin' of your mother, where is she?

BETTY. Gone to the County Ball.

WILLIAM. Oh, I'd forgotten; it's tonight.

SALLY. You've just missed the grand parade. She went accompanied by two men.

WILLIAM (*laughing*) Did she now? A chip of the old block, havin' the men waitin' on her, like I had the women after me. (*He takes out a pipe and pouch and fills his pipe*)

BETTY. I've heard about you and your heart affairs.

WILLIAM. It's a wonder I have any heart left at all; it's been that busy in my lifetime. And what would it be you're wantin' to see me for?

BOB. It's about Mother.

WILLIAM. I'd an idea it might be. Actin' strange-like, isn't she?

SALLY. I'd almost say she was going kittenish if it was anyone else.

WILLIAM. And if she is, what's the objection? If the old tabby finds her rompin' days are not quite over, what's wrong in that?

BOB. We want to know why Mother's suddenly changed, and also—what is more important—where's it going to end?

WILLIAM. Ah now, you've put a poser. I'll have to get my thinkin' cap on, and I could do a lot better if I had just a drop of encouragement, but in this house you're not so well-mannered to your guests.

(Bob *smiles and moves up* C, *thus exposing the whisky decanter on the table*)

Hospitality is an art . . . (*He stops, stares hard at the table and gasps*) Holy smoke! Are my old eyes playin' me tricks? What is it I see yonder? (*He rises*)

BETTY. I think it's whisky; would you like some, Grandy?

WILLIAM. Would I? Aren't there some unnecessary questions asked in this world? (*He moves to the table*) God bless you, Robert, for your kindly thought. (*He pours himself out a drink*)

BOB. It's not me, it's Mother's doings.

WILLIAM (*adding more whisky to his glass*) I see now she's a reformed character, like you said. (*He moves to the armchair* RC *and holds up the glass*) This might give me inspiration.

SALLY (*moving to the table*) Shall I bring the syphon?

WILLIAM. You wouldn't be wantin' to spoil a good drink? (*He drinks and sits in the armchair*) Ah, now we can ponder with a refreshed mind.

BOB (*moving down to* L *of William*) Grandy, can you tell us what Mother is up to? And what's made her so different? She's even showing generosity!

WILLIAM (*anxiously*) What, with money?

BETTY. She gave me a hundred pounds three weeks ago. I'd never seen more than five at a time in my life before.

SALLY. She actually bought a new pram for baby, and without being asked.

BOB. And she gave me an extra allowance; small, but very useful; and the same for Peter.

WILLIAM. Now's the time, it seems, for me to have my allowance increased, before the generous impulse dies away again!

BOB. That's only part. She's spending on herself; she's going out, dressing herself up . . .

WILLIAM (*holding up his hand*) Shush, my boy! I know it all! I know the signs like a doctor knows the sign of some malignant disease. But this is no disease, unless you call love a disease!

BOB. Love? Don't talk rot!

WILLIAM. I say "love" and I mean it. In some way I may be the one responsible, for I had a serious word with your mother some weeks ago.

BETTY (*rising and moving to* R *of William*) You think she's fallen in love? Seems extraordinary for Mother, and at her age!

WILLIAM. What's age got to do with it? Whether they're nineteen or ninety makes no odds. I know myself I was as good as ever up to sixty-five, and even now my heart can go pitter-patter at times . . .

BOB. It's impossible to imagine Mother . . .

WILLIAM. Just because it's your own mother. If you heard of anyone else you'd smile, but you'd believe it. So why not your own mother? After all, she's young yet.

SALLY (*moving to* L *of Bob*) So you think she's in love with someone?

WILLIAM. I'm not sayin' that. I wouldn't say she's already marked out her victim, but I think she's made up her mind she'll have another go at marriage, and with a determined woman like her, somebody's doomed.

BETTY. Grandy, you may be right. (*She sits at the left end of the sofa*) It's a question of whom she'll marry.

WILLIAM. That's a detail. Just get used to the idea she's goin' to do it.

BOB (*crossing to the fireplace*) If Mother's marrying again, we want a say in the matter.

WILLIAM. Would you prefer to choose the man yourself, and save her the trouble?

BETTY. Don't be silly, Bob. We can't do anything about it, and why should we want to?

SALLY. It's all very well for you, Betty, but for Bob and me it matters. If your mother marries, this man might take over the business control. Then what about poor Bob?

WILLIAM. Ah, you're crossin' your bridges before they come to you. They used to say, "find the woman"; I say to you, "find the man", and then do the talkin'.

BOB. You mean, find who she's going to marry?

WILLIAM. Certainly. She must have a kind of short list of likely ones. I know one or two myself.

SALLY. Yes, so do we.

WILLIAM. And the hot favourite would seem to be that new fella who set up recently with the electric works.

BOB. That's right. Harry Bateman.

SALLY. But he's much younger than she, must be seven or eight years.

WILLIAM. A mere trifle to these amorous women, my girl. He's a smart, go-ahead, likely man. What would you say, Elizabeth?

BETTY (*non-committally*) I suppose he's in the running.

BOB. If she married him, Heaven help us! He'd want to run the whole works and us as well.

SALLY (*moving* L; *thoughtfully*) She's very friendly with Mr Yardley.

BOB. Yardley's the family solicitor, known him for years.

BETTY. Does it rule him out?

BOB. No, but he's an old man, must be sixty. I wouldn't consider Yardley.

WILLIAM (*rising, moving to the table and pouring himself another drink*) If the woman's on the warpath, you must consider every man, likely and unlikely.

BOB. It beats me why she started all this manhunting.

WILLIAM. I dropped out a word to her, and thought it might do her good to consider marrying again. (*He raises his glass to drink*)

BOB. You've started something, and you might suffer yourself. (*He crosses to William*) Suppose the new husband made her cut your allowance?

WILLIAM (*spluttering over his drink*) What a terrible thought! Robert, don't put the fear into me like that.

BOB. Well, it's possible.

WILLIAM. It is indeed. That would be a terrible disaster, and after my kindly suggestions, too.

BETTY (*rising*) Perhaps she won't marry after all.

WILLIAM. She's got the bit between her teeth now, and she'll go on like a horse in sight of the winning-post. (*He pauses*) Elizabeth, which of her suitors do you think would be likely to be kind to an old gentleman in his declining years? (*He fills up his glass from the decanter*)

SALLY. Bob, I think you and Betty and Peter should ask your mother how you stand if she does this.

BETTY (*sitting on the left arm of the sofa*) Utterly futile. We should be told to mind our own business.

WILLIAM. You're all talking round and round in circles. You can't stop your mother from marryin' if she's set on it, but at least you can try to get her to marry the man who'll suit you best.

BOB (*crossing to the fireplace*) Harry Bateman won't suit us, and he's the likely one.

WILLIAM. Then why don't you see she doesn't marry him? (*He drains the last drop of whisky from the decanter into his glass and drinks*)

SALLY. How?

WILLIAM. Ah, you've got to meet cunnin' with cunnin'. (*He holds up the empty decanter and turns it upside down*) If you don't mind I'll be leavin' you, or I'll be late for my business appointment. (*He moves up* LC *towards the door, then turns*) There's an old sayin', "set a thief to catch a thief", I would say, "set a woman to catch a woman".

BOB. I don't get that.

WILLIAM. Your sister Elizabeth has a knowin' look in her eye. She's an intelligent girl. Good night to ye all.

WILLIAM *winks at them and exits up* LC *as—*

the CURTAIN *falls*

The CURTAIN *is lowered for a minute only, to denote the passing of a few hours.*
When the CURTAIN *rises the time is almost 2 a.m. The room is lighted by the standard lamp and looks cosy and inviting. The fire is still glowing.* VICTORIA *enters up* LC, *followed by* HARRY.

VICTORIA. Come in, Harry. Have a cigarette and a drink before you go.

HARRY. Thanks. (*He helps Victoria off with her coat and lays it on the chair* R *of the door*)

VICTORIA (*crossing to the fire and warming her hands*) Nice to get back, but I could have gone on even longer. Doesn't time simply fly? Nearly two o'clock, feels more like eleven. (*She sits at the right end of the sofa, and stretches out her arms, looking radiant*)

HARRY (*moving to her*) The night is but young . . .

VICTORIA. But the clock tells us otherwise. (*She smiles up at him*) Have you really enjoyed yourself, Harry?

HARRY. Tremendously. Thank you so much.

VICTORIA. Whatever for?

HARRY. You've helped to make the evening. (*He sits beside her on the sofa*) I'm a stranger in these parts. You dance particularly well, you know.

VICTORIA. I'm out of practice. I was terribly nervous.

HARRY. I'd make anybody nervous, tripping and treading on you like an elephant. You're very long-suffering to stand me.

VICTORIA. Not a bit; I can stand a lot of what I like.

HARRY. Thank you. Then I haven't monopolised you too much tonight?

VICTORIA. I wasn't aware you were monopolising me. Perhaps I was so unconsciously happy . . .

HARRY. You're being very nice to me, or just pulling my leg. I'm not sure which.

VICTORIA (*seriously*) I'm not pulling your leg.

(*There is a pause as they exchange looks*)

I wonder where Grace and John are; I thought they were on our heels. (*She jumps up*) Let's have a cigarette. (*She takes a box of cigarettes from the mantelpiece*)

HARRY (*rising*) John had trouble in getting his car away. Somebody holding him up, I think.

(VICTORIA *takes a cigarette herself and offers the box to Harry*)

Oh, thanks, Vicky.

VICTORIA. John's a grand sort.

HARRY. And a great admirer of yours. (*He lights Victoria's cigarette and then his own from his lighter*)

VICTORIA. We're old friends, almost grown up together. (*She sits at the right end of the sofa*)

HARRY (*sitting beside her*) Perhaps John won't feel like calling round at this time. He may want to go straight off home to bed.

VICTORIA. Not old John. (*She smiles*) He likes a late party, and besides, I asked them to call.

HARRY (*quietly*) Oh.

VICTORIA. Why that "Oh"?

HARRY. Well, to tell the truth, I was thinking how nice and cosy it is here, quietly chatting.

VICTORIA. I was thinking the same. It's so peaceful. I feel like a spoiled cat relaxing in the warmth and cosiness of it all.

HARRY (*hesitantly*) Vicky, do you think I could stay on a few minutes, just to have a little chat with you?

VICTORIA. That means pushing Grace and John off. I don't know whether I can, and whether I ought to.

HARRY. No, it might seem a bit odd, but I only thought it . . .

VICTORIA. I'll see about it.

(*The sound of a car is heard off*)

(*She rises*) I think they're here now. I'd better go and open the door for them. (*She moves up to the door* LC)

(HARRY *rises and stands by the fireplace*)

(*She pauses at the door*) Am I wise in letting you stay on?

HARRY. What's the harm?

VICTORIA. As you say, "what's the harm?" (*She smiles, switches on the lights by the switch at the door and goes out*)

(*She returns almost immediately, followed by* GRACE *and* JOHN)

JOHN. Some damn fool left his car right in front of mine; had to wait till he came out. (*He takes off his coat and puts it on the chair* R *of the door*)

GRACE (*walking painfully down* C) Let me get to a chair. My feet feel like suet puddings. (*She sinks into the armchair* RC) I'm slipping my shoes off.

VICTORIA (*moving to* L *of Grace*) You'll never get them on again, Grace.

GRACE. I'll chance that. It's a luxury to get 'em off. (*She kicks off both her shoes*) Ooh, what a relief! Folks with good feet don't know how well off they are.

VICTORIA (*looking at Harry*) I'm sure you men would like a drink before you go.

GRACE. So would I, I'm fair gaspin'.

VICTORIA. John, would you help yourselves.

JOHN (*moving to the table*) Thank you, Victoria. I won't say "No". Come on, Harry, you'd better join me.

HARRY (*crossing to* R *of John*) I don't mind if I do.

(JOHN *begins to pour out the drinks*)

GRACE. Mine's a drop of port, as usual.

JOHN. And you, Victoria?

VICTORIA. On this occasion I'll have a little port.

GRACE. Going gay, Vicky.

JOHN. Here, Harry, hand the ladies their glasses.

(HARRY *hands a glass of port to Grace, then one to Victoria.* VICTORIA *sits on the left arm of the armchair* RC)

Now we'll have a decent man's drink. Here you are, Harry. (*He hands Harry a tot of whisky*)

GRACE. Well, here's to us all, and many more doos like to-night.

(*They all raise their glasses and drink*)

JOHN. Very good affair, I think. Of course it always is. (*He sits* L *of the table*) Enjoyed yourself, Harry?

HARRY. I certainly have. Looking forward to the next. (*He sits* R *of the table*)

JOHN. Haven't seen much of you tonight, Victoria. Every time I looked for you, you were missing.

GRACE. But not neglected, I'll bet.

VICTORIA. Oh no, I haven't been lonely.

JOHN. You wouldn't know many there, Harry. Afraid it might have been boring for you?

HARRY. On the contrary, I've never known the time go so fast.

JOHN. Oh well, that's all right then. Wouldn't like to think you were out of it.

GRACE (*looking very hard at Victoria*) I should say he was very much in it.

JOHN (*to Grace*) You've done yourself well tonight.

GRACE. I've done my feet in! But it's worth it. I've had every dance whether I could do 'em or not, and I'll bet my partners' feet are feeling the scars of battle as well as mine.

JOHN. Thank God I didn't meet you, Grace.

VICTORIA. Just look at the time. Two o'clock.

GRACE. That's all right, nobody's worrying.

JOHN. You're right, Grace, what does it matter? With your permission, Victoria, I'll have just a wee drop more.

VICTORIA. Of course, help yourself.

JOHN. Thanks. (*He rises and picks up the decanter*) Come on, Harry, just a drop 'ere we depart.

HARRY. Thanks, just a spot.

(*While JOHN pours out the drinks, VICTORIA mutters quickly to GRACE who grins and shows that she realizes what Victoria wants. VICTORIA rises and moves to the fireplace*)

GRACE (*holding out her glass*) John, I'll have a small quick final and off I'll go.

(*HARRY rises and takes her glass. JOHN pours out a drink*)

I wish I could leave my feet here. Wouldn't it be nice if you could put your tired feet to bed, and the rest of you stay up late?

JOHN (*handing her the drink*) Tight shoes, that's why you've got bad feet.

GRACE (*taking the drink*) I've spent half my life trying to wear fours when I know I should take sixes. (*She drinks*)

(*JOHN puts her empty glass on the table*)

Well, let's be makin' a move. I'll put my shoes on, if I can. (*She bends down and eases one foot into her shoe*) Ooh, it's murder! (*She stops and looks at them*) Let me get my breath.

JOHN. Come here, let me try. (*He makes a move as if to help her*)

GRACE. Do you fancy yourself as the Prince fitting Cinderella's slipper?

(*They all laugh*)

I'll have another go. (*She bends down and eases the other foot into her shoe*) Ha, just managed it! (*She rises*) Now that I'm on my feet, I'm goin'. John, I like your car, plenty of room in it. It's not one of those little courtin' cars. Suppose you drop me off?

JOHN. Yes, with pleasure, Grace, but to be strictly precise, I'm a little off your route. Harry passes your door. You'd give her a lift, Harry?

HARRY (*expressionless*) Yes, of course.

VICTORIA. I was thinking, if anyone saw you, it might look rather odd. Grace and Harry are comparative strangers; we wouldn't like to have our Grace compromised!

JOHN (*roaring with laughter*) Grace compromised? That's funny.

GRACE. And what's so funny about it? Do you think I'm past bein' compromised? (*She moves to R of John*)

VICTORIA (*moving RC*) It would be more diplomatic if you dropped her, John.

JOHN. Well, as a matter of fact, I wanted to stay behind a few moments to have a word with you—business, you know.

VICTORIA. That would do tomorrow.

JOHN. 'Fraid not. I'm off to London on the nine-twenty.

VICTORIA. But it can wait until you're back . . .

GRACE (*loudly*) If you've made up your minds who's conveying me home, we'll start.

JOHN. Hope you don't mind, Harry. (*He crosses decisively to the fireplace and warms his hands*) I must have a word with Victoria to-night, as I'm away till tomorrow. Business must go on, you know.

HARRY. That's all right. If you're ready, Grace . . . ?

GRACE. You've finished fighting over me, then? Come on, let's get off. (*She looks at Victoria*) You can't get the best of a solicitor. Good night, Vicky. Good night, John. Oh, my feet, they feel like balloons. (*She limps up to the door LC*)

HARRY (*to Victoria*) Good night, Vicky. Thanks again for a lovely evening. May I call sometime?

VICTORIA (*smiling at him*) My house is always open to you, Harry.

HARRY. Thanks. Good night. (*He moves up to the door. To Grace*) I'd better carry you to the car.

GRACE. You'd better not, unless you want to break your back.

(HARRY *and* GRACE *exit up* LC, *laughing.* VICTORIA, *rather annoyed at Harry's departure, turns to John*)

VICTORIA. I really should go off to bed, John, unless there's something important.

JOHN. There is.

VICTORIA. I hope there's nothing wrong; we've had such a lovely time tonight.

JOHN. No, nothing wrong. I've enjoyed myself, too. (*He moves to Victoria*) The only snag, I didn't see much of you. Harry kept you to himself.

VICTORIA. I enjoyed his company. Don't you like him, John?

JOHN. Don't know much about him to pass an opinion. Seems a decent sort, but something of a ladies' man from all accounts.

Fond of you, apparently. In fact, if I didn't know you as well as I do, I might even start thinking things. But as it is, it makes me smile.

VICTORIA. Makes you smile, does it? (*She moves* R *to the fireplace*) You've still got your sense of humour, John.

JOHN. Harry's a harmless sort of chap. Probably flattered by our friendliness to him, as he's a newcomer in the town. (*He sits on the right arm of the armchair* RC) It wouldn't be fair to get wrong ideas about him, as far as you're concerned, I mean. Besides, I should think he's only about forty—well, not much more; can't be.

VICTORIA (*perturbed*) What is the pressing business, John? What have we to discuss at this time of night?

JOHN (*smiling*) Not business really. Just you. I'll be honest, and admit I tricked you into letting me stay a few moments.

VICTORIA. You're puzzling me.

JOHN. Victoria, I want to speak frankly and sincerely. When I say you've altered recently, I am not telling you anything you don't know already. I'm not going to ask your reason, and I'm not going to speculate on what this change will mean to you, but I want to say something else if I may.

VICTORIA (*interested*) If you wish. (*She sits at the right end of the sofa*)

JOHN (*rising and moving to* L *of the sofa*) I've been watching you for the past month, and particularly tonight, when I was permitted, (*with a grin*) and I thought what a pretty picture you made; slim, youthful, with a kind of elusive charm I cannot easily describe.

VICTORIA. How very sweet of you, John.

JOHN. Oh, I meant it. Tonight there wasn't a more attractive woman in the place. Dammit, you made the young girls look silly. (*He sits beside her on the sofa*)

VICTORIA. Nice of you to think so, but it still doesn't make me any less than fifty.

JOHN. Thirty or fifty, I'm telling you what effect you're making. And I thought, *what a woman*, and wasting her life with a blessed factory and a grown-up family.

VICTORIA. What could I do better?

JOHN. I'll tell you. You could marry again. Haven't you ever considered the idea?

VICTORIA. I hadn't until quite recently.

JOHN. Then you *are* thinking of it?

VICTORIA. Thinking of it, and intending to do it may be quite different. Shall we say the idea of marriage has crossed my mind, as my children don't need me any longer . . . ?

JOHN. Yes, that's so. (*He rises and moves* C) And as they grow up you are left alone more and more. Loneliness is a terrible thing, Victoria. To elderly people it looms like a dark cloud. You may have money, a lovely home and good health, but what's the use of it all if you're lonely?

VICTORIA. It's a terrifying thought.

JOHN (*turning to her*) Then you would consider marrying again?

VICTORIA. For the first time in eighteen years I have breathing time to think of myself. I've suddenly wakened up to the fact that life's going on swiftly. I'm getting older, and if I'm to have a second lease of life, I must do it quickly.

JOHN. You've said it all for me. When a woman's young, she needs caring for, and when she's middle-aged and left, as you are, she needs protection.

VICTORIA. I never knew I needed protecting, but I think I know what you mean. To put it in ordinary language—it's nice to have a man about the house. (*She smiles broadly*)

JOHN (*moving to L of the sofa; earnestly*) Victoria, I've known you from the time your husband died; that's a long time now, and I've watched you bring up a family and care for the business in a way I've admired and respected. You're a very wonderful woman, you know.

VICTORIA. I've simply done the job I was left to do, that's all.

JOHN (*sitting beside her*) Have you ever thought how much we have in common? You've been paddling along on your own all these years, and for the past ten years I've been alone. It isn't right. I've come to that conclusion.

VICTORIA. I've often wondered why you didn't marry again, John.

JOHN. There's been one very good reason—the right woman never appeared, or to be more correct, I should say I had the right woman in mind, but never dared approach her.

VICTORIA. Faint heart . . . You know that saying?

JOHN. Victoria, can't you see what I'm driving at? I'm wondering if you'd consider marrying me?

VICTORIA (*rising; really surprised*) John!

JOHN. This isn't a sudden idea, but until recently I haven't felt I could approach you. You've confessed you wouldn't rule out marrying again.

VICTORIA (*staring in front of her and thinking hard*) Yes, I know.

JOHN. Then let's try it, my dear. (*He rises and stands L of her*) We know one another, and that's something, isn't it? I don't know how you feel about me, but I've had nothing but love and adoration for you for years.

VICTORIA. I've always liked you, John.

JOHN. Do you like me enough to marry me? That's the point.

VICTORIA. That's what I'm wondering.

JOHN. Perhaps I've spoken at the wrong time. After all, it's hardly fair to say this at two o'clock in the morning, or is it? Some people would say it's just the hour.

VICTORIA. It's awfully sweet of you, John. I take it as a lovely compliment.

JOHN. But you're not saying you will? Victoria, be frank with me, and if I've blundered, tell me so, and as they say—I'll take it.

(*There is a pause*)

Aren't you going to say anything?

VICTORIA (*turning to him; very gently*) I think perhaps you'd better go.

JOHN (*rather sadly*) I think I had. It's getting late, and I'm off in the morning to London. (*Brightly; smiling*) I wonder whether Harry dropped old Grace safely, with her bad feet. Ah well, it's been a grand night. Good night Victoria, my dear. (*He kisses her hand, then moves up and picks up his coat*)

VICTORIA (*moving up to him at the door*) Good night, John dear.

JOHN *opens the door as—*

the CURTAIN *falls*

ACT III

SCENE—*The same. One week later. Evening.*
The curtains are drawn, all the lights are on, and the room looks even more attractive than before.

When the CURTAIN *rises* SALLY *is sitting in the chair* R *of the table, sewing.* BOB *enters up* LC.

BOB. I've just been phoning Mr Yardley. Mother wants him urgently tonight. He wanted to know what she wanted, and all I could say was that I didn't know, but it was important. (*He crosses to the fireplace*)
SALLY. And your grandpa's coming too, isn't he?
BOB. He is.

(PETER *enters up* LC, *smoking a cigarette*)

PETER (*moving down* C) What's all this commotion? I intended going out, but I've been told Mother wants to see us.
BOB. Quite correct. We're to stay in; the old man's coming up, and Yardley as well.
PETER. Complete mobilization of the family, eh?
BOB. That's about it. And don't ask me why, because I don't know.
PETER. Mother's so infernally secretive, nobody ever knows anything until the very last second; but there's something mighty important in the wind.
SALLY. She's not in financial trouble, is she, Bob?

(BOB *and* PETER *laugh at this*)

BOB. That's the last trouble she can be in.
PETER (*leaning on the back of the armchair* RC) I know. She's going to sell out, that's why we're all being told, and that's why the solicitor has to come.
BOB. I wonder. There's been no hint of it, but with Mother you can never tell.
PETER. How do we stand if she's going to do that? (*Despondently*) Less hope than ever of my getting married. (*He sits on the left arm of the armchair* RC)
SALLY. You are a couple of sillies! Your mother's a business woman. She'd never dream of selling out. Just use your imagination if you have any, and put two and two together.

BOB. Well, Mrs Clever, as we're such duffers, please tell us. (*He moves to* R *of the armchair* RC)

SALLY. It means simply one thing. She's going to get married again, and she's making an official announcement to the family.

PETER. Do you know that as a fact? Is she really, Sally?

BOB. She doesn't know, she's guessing. Favourite pastime of women, guessing who's going to marry whom.

SALLY. All right. You'll see.

PETER. She may be right, Bob.

(BETTY *enters up* LC, *looking very smart*)

What if the old girl is going to do it?

BETTY (*moving* C) And what old girl is under discussion, may I ask?

BOB. Mother. I suppose you know there's a family meeting tonight?

BETTY (*crossing to the fireplace; looking pleased*) I've had due notice, and intend to be present. It should be fun.

PETER. You look very smug and self-satisfied; like the cat that's just had the cream.

BETTY. Not at all, but I'm not going to worry myself like you two. You look as if you've come to the reading of Mother's will, and she's going to cut you both right out!

PETER. And you're dolled up as if you're the chief benefici—whatever they call it. Isn't she looking a glamour piece tonight, Bob? Why, you don't look a day above thirty, Betty.

BETTY (*coldly*) I am twenty-nine. (*She sits in the armchair down* R)

BOB (*sitting on the left arm of the sofa*) Sally thinks this is a gathering of the clan for Mother to announce a forthcoming marriage, as the papers would say.

BETTY. Oh, that's your theory, Sally?

SALLY. Well, you've known for some time that your mother might one day marry again. What do you think, Betty?

BETTY. I've no theories. I'll just wait and see.

PETER (*slipping down into the armchair*) There's one point you don't mention, the small matter of our new step-father. If you're right, Sally, who's the lucky man?

SALLY (*going on with her sewing*) Harry Bateman, of course.

PETER. But she hardly knows him.

BOB. Does it matter? At any rate she's seen enough of him in the past month or so.

PETER. Then he must have already popped the question. When did this happen?

BOB. We don't know. We don't even know the question has been popped at all. Ask Sally. She seems to be the knowing one.

SALLY. I didn't say I knew, but I have eyes and ears.

PETER. But that fellow Bateman's years younger than Mother.

BETTY. I believe he's forty-three, to be precise.

BOB. Of course, he's on a good thing—money; at least that's what he's after.

BETTY. Is he? You talk as if you knew, Bob.

BOB. It's clear enough. (*He rises*) He's been flattering Mother and fussing round her. He's also been fussing round you and even been polite to me, all with one object, to get well in. And Mother's been lapping it up. After being cooped up so quietly for years, all this has gone to her head.

PETER. That's about the size of it. Don't you agree, Betty?

BETTY. How would I know?

SALLY. You've seen something of Mr Bateman, Betty. In fact, you know him better than any of us.

BETTY. I was just thinking the same thing.

BOB. Well, hasn't he confided in you?

BETTY (*sounding almost bored*) And if he has? I'm not likely to tell you.

PETER. Our secretive sister! I'll bet she knows plenty. Come on, Betty, let's have it!

BETTY. Better ask Mother!

(BOB *moves to the fireplace.*
HETTY *enters up* LC, *looking concerned and ready for trouble*)

HETTY. Pardon me, Mr Robert, I thought your mother was here, but as she's not, you'll do. (*She crosses to Bob*)

BOB. What is it?

HETTY. I understand I have to stay up tonight till ten o'clock. Bit of a party on, haven't you?

BOB. Hardly a party, but what's the trouble?

HETTY. I can't do it. My Union won't let me.

BOB. Union? *You* mustn't talk about Unions.

HETTY. And why not? Don't I need protection from the capitalist classes like your workers do? I came here, as your mother was at her wits' end for help, and she said she'd give me the same as I was getting in the hotel.

BOB. Well, isn't she?

HETTY. Yes, she is, but she also agreed that I should have the same conditions for work as in the hotel.

BOB. Haven't you?

HETTY. That I have not, and the first thing I have to remember is loyalty to my Union. Our Secretary says that's the first lesson we must learn. Whether we think it right or wrong, we must stand fast to the Union.

BOB. What *is* all this?

HETTY. I say I can't work till ten, 'cos my spread-over would be put wrong.

BETTY. Your spread-over, Hetty?

HETTY. My daily hours have to be spread over fourteen hours of the day. This mornin' I started off at seven, and seven till nine is fourteen hours. If I go on till ten it's wrong, and what would my Union say?

PETER. Would they know?

HETTY. It's not a case of "would they know?" but of principles. Our Secretary says we always keep to the principles, and our first duty is to be a loyal servant of the Union.

BOB. What about being a loyal servant to my mother? Are you going to quibble about a trifling thing when you know quite well that if there's extra money to be paid, you'll have it?

HETTY. Our Secretary's warned us about persuasion, and I mustn't listen to you, in case I'm won over.

BOB. And suppose I said my mother could get half a dozen girls like you, and you can go to blazes with your spread-over, what would your Secretary call that?

HETTY. That would be intimidation, and he's told us not to stand for any hanky-panky of that sort.

PETER. That Secretary seems to have covered every possible contingency.

(VICTORIA *enters up* LC, *looking as attractive and youthful as ever in a new frock. She has taken pains to look her best. She sweeps in and sees Hetty*)

VICTORIA. Oh, Hetty, I wanted to see you. We've one or two visitors coming tonight. My father will be here shortly. Show him into the dining-room. And I expect Mr Yardley. You can take him into the dining-room, too. When Mr Bateman calls, which he may do at any moment, please show him in here. (*She moves down* L *to the desk*)

HETTY. I was comin' to see you, Mrs Anson. I've got a grievance. My hours today are interfering with my spread-over.

VICTORIA. Your what? Oh, I know what you mean. That's all right, don't bother me now. (*She turns over the papers on the desk*) If you're worried, we'll settle it at ten shillings. Will that do?

HETTY (*delighted*) Oh, yes, thank you, Mrs Anson. I'll work till midnight if you like. You are kind.

PETER. What would the Union Secretary call that—bribery?

HETTY (*moving up to the door* LC) He says it isn't bribery if you're in complete agreement.

(HETTY *exits up* LC)

VICTORIA. Now I'd better go and finish dressing properly. (*She looks round and takes notice of the others for the first time*) How nice to see my children round their own fireside. (*She moves* C)

PETER. But you *asked* us to stay in tonight, Mother.

VICTORIA. So I did. (*Pleasantly*) I do hope I haven't inconvenienced any of you. But it *is* rather special tonight. You're going to be *very* interested and, I think, very pleased, before the night's over.

BOB. Mother, you're very mysterious.

VICTORIA. Ah, Woman is ever mysterious, Robert.

(*Smiling,* VICTORIA *moves up* LC *and exits*)

BOB. Well, what do you make of that?

PETER. You hear what she says, that chap Bateman's coming. (*He rises and moves* L)

SALLY. What did I tell you?

BETTY. It may be a purely social call.

BOB. Mother's got it all cut and dried. She's worked it out like a railway timetable, even to the moment of the big announcement.

SALLY. Did you notice she was wearing another new dress? Now perhaps you'll believe me. And did you notice how radiant she was; and almost purring?

(*The sound of the front-door bell is heard off*)

BOB. Here's the man of the moment! We'd better vanish.

PETER. Wait a second. It may be Grandpa.

(HETTY *enters up* LC *and shows in* WILLIAM)

WILLIAM. Ah, good evenin' to ye all.

HETTY. Mrs Anson said I was to show you to the dining-room.

WILLIAM. There's no hurry. I'll find my way when I've greeted my relations. (*He moves down to* L *of the armchair* RC)

(HETTY *shrugs her shoulders and exits up* LC)

It's a rare pleasure to see you all gathered around. There's a reason for it, just as there is for having me comin' up here tonight.

BETTY. Yes, Grandy, Mother wants to meet the family. (*She rises and moves to* R *of the armchair* RC)

WILLIAM. What's she goin' to say? Is she presentin' Armistice terms?

PETER. That fellow, Harry Bateman is expected any moment. (*He turns the desk chair round to face* C *and sits*)

WILLIAM (*laughing*) Oh, then the hot favourite is romping home? (*He sits on the left arm of the armchair*)

BOB. You won't laugh when he gets installed here and starts throwing his weight about. He's a business man.

WILLIAM. Ooch, I don't like the breed, all discipline and authority. No good Irishman ever knuckles under to authority. I never did, and I'll not start now. He'd be expectin' me to live within my income.

BETTY (*mockingly*) No, Grandy!

WILLIAM. He would indeed, he'd stoop as low as that. If your poor mother gets tied up to a man of that kind, she's a lost soul, and so am I.

D

SALLY (*rising*) Bob, I think I'll go upstairs and see if the child's all right.

(SALLY *exits up* LC)

WILLIAM (*rising and moving* L) I was thinking, if your mother's determined to tread this miserable path with this man, what's the point of demanding my presence tonight? There's enough misery without insisting on me staying to listen to it.

BOB. She's something to tell us all—you included.

PETER. Mr Yardley, the solicitor, is coming.

WILLIAM. That's a bad sign, it bodes no good to have such a man around. She'll be havin' him to make a settlement of marriage on this fella, and that'll leave me high and dry. And mention of the word "dry" causes me to remove myself to your dining-room (*he moves to the door* L) where, if my memory serves me right, I'll find a little consolation.

BETTY (*crossing to William*) There's a full decanter waiting for you, Grandy.

WILLIAM. Thank ye, my girl. If they all had a heart like you, your poor old grandfather wouldn't be sufferin' as he is.

(BETTY *and* WILLIAM *exit* L)

PETER (*rising*) Not much help from the old man.

BOB. He started all this, and he doesn't care; we've got the worry. I tell you this, Peter, I'll have it out with Bateman, and if he thinks by marrying Mother he's going to run the whole business, he's sadly mistaken.

PETER (*moving up to the door* L; *persuasively*) Come on, what's the use of talking? Let's go out before the great lover arrives.

BOB (*crossing to Peter; grumbling*) I don't know why Mother wants to bother about marrying again. It's an infernal nuisance to everybody. She should be more considerate.

(BOB *and* PETER *exit* L. *The sound of the front-door bell is heard off.*

HETTY *enters up* LC *and ushers in* HARRY BATEMAN. *He looks nervous and seems relieved when he finds that he is alone. He stands* C)

HETTY. Please wait here, Mr Bateman. Mrs Anson's expecting you. I'll go and tell her. (*She turns to go*)

(VICTORIA *enters up* LC)

VICTORIA. I heard the bell and guessed who it was.

(HETTY *exits up* LC)

(*She moves down to Harry*) Nice to see you, Harry. Do sit down. (*She sits on the chair* L *of the table*)

HARRY (*sitting* R *of the table*) Thanks, Vicky. It's good to see you again.

VICTORIA. Do you know you've been a whole week away from us? I've been expecting you every day.

HARRY. Well, I've been out of town and very busy. This is really the first leisure moment for days. I've been wanting to come, believe me.

VICTORIA. All right, you're forgiven. I wondered if the Ball last week had been too much for you?

HARRY. No fear. I could manage that sort of thing every week.

VICTORIA. It *was* rather nice, I agree. I've never been able to apologize for having to let you go that night, Harry. You did want to stay a little longer, didn't you?

HARRY. Yes, I did. (*Embarrassed*) In fact, I've really come to talk now of what I should have mentioned, or asked, that night.

VICTORIA (*rising and crossing to the armchair* RC; *eagerly*) Oh? You haven't forgotten what you wanted to say, even after a week's business?

HARRY. This is too important to forget. In fact, it's vital to me.

VICTORIA (*lightly; but delighted*) What a serious man you've become all at once. (*She sits in the armchair*) But I'm interrupting.

HARRY. Vicky, I came to your town only a few months ago, a stranger, and I felt very lonely, but not for long, thanks to you and your family and a few others.

VICTORIA. What have we done? Only tried to make you welcome.

HARRY (*rising*) You've done a great deal, Vicky. You've taken me around, given me hospitality and a great deal of happiness. To put it mildly, you've been tremendously kind.

VICTORIA. I wasn't aware I'd done *so* much. But if I have, I suppose it's because I like you, Harry.

HARRY. And I like you too, Vicky. I did, right from first coming here.

VICTORIA. To meet someone one likes is a rare pleasure, all too rare these days, especially for me. I think you know how I've lived—within myself—for years. Making friends hasn't come to me easily.

HARRY. Thanks. (*He moves to Victoria*) I appreciate the compliment—*and* the friendship. But friendship can lead to something more, and that's what makes it terribly hard to explain.

VICTORIA. Harry, what *are* you trying to say?

HARRY. Well, Vicky, I'd hate you to think I'm trying to take advantage for my own ends. You're looking puzzled, so I might as well say it. I'm thinking about marriage. (*He sits on the left arm of the armchair*)

VICTORIA (*pleased*) Oh.

HARRY. Does it surprise you?

VICTORIA. Well—er—I don't quite know.

HARRY. Perhaps you thought I was a confirmed bachelor? I

never thought about marriage, not seriously anyhow, until quite recently. But now I've made up my mind, and I think there's nothing like it. I must have needed the right woman to come along.

VICTORIA. And has she?

HARRY (*smiling*) She has.

VICTORIA. And you're quite sure you want to?

HARRY. I'm certain; never been so sure of anything in my life. (*He leans over her slightly*)

VICTORIA (*teasing*) Would I know her, Harry?

HARRY. If *you* don't, no-one does.

VICTORIA. Harry, *what are you* trying to say?

HARRY. Vicky, I want your permission to marry Betty.

(*There is a pause*)

VICTORIA (*faintly*) You—what?

HARRY. I'm in love with your daughter Betty, and I'd like to marry her.

VICTORIA (*rising; bewildered*) You love Betty?

HARRY. I knew it would surprise you, but I hoped I wouldn't give you too much of a shock.

(*There is a pause*)

I am afraid I have. (*He rises*)

VICTORIA (*trying bravely to smile*) Forgive me, Harry, if I look a bit dazed, but it is something of a surprise.

HARRY. You didn't suspect anything?

VICTORIA (*in a sardonic tone*) I never suspected what you've told me.

HARRY (*pleased*) I told Betty you wouldn't ever guess. I think we've been clever in keeping it quiet.

VICTORIA (*dully*) Very clever.

HARRY. I wanted to mention it at least a week ago, but never got the chance, so I was determined to confess tonight. (*He smiles*) She's a grand girl, Vicky. I'm lucky to find her unmarried and unattached. Somebody's been slow around here.

VICTORIA (*sitting at the right end of the sofa; in a lifeless tone*) Betty has always lived a quiet life.

HARRY. Then it's high time she started married life, and with your permission, Vicky, may I have that honour? (*He moves to* L *of the sofa*)

VICTORIA. It is perhaps unnecessary to ask if Betty's in love with you.

HARRY. According to what she says, she certainly is. Of course, there's a bit of difference in age. I'm forty-three, and Betty's not thirty, but perhaps I don't seem *very* old. Would you think I'm old, Vicky? (*He sits on the arm of the sofa*)

VICTORIA (*quietly*) You've always seemed young to me, Harry.

HARRY. One good thing about it, the age business is the right way round. The trouble seems to start when the woman's older than the man. (*He pauses*) Anyway, Betty seems willing to try me.

VICTORIA. Then what is there for me to say? (*She turns away*)

HARRY. Oh, just to give the formal parental blessing. Betty wanted to break it to you, but I said it was my place, especially as you'd been so nice to me.

VICTORIA. Very chivalrous of you.

HARRY. I haven't mentioned my financial position, but I'm quite capable of supporting a wife in a decent way.

VICTORIA. We won't question that.

HARRY. I only mention it as some people are quick to suspect a man who wants to marry a girl from a wealthy family.

VICTORIA. Betty isn't wealthy. In fact, she has nothing. (*She smiles oddly*) I have the money in this house. (*She rises and moves to the fireplace*)

HARRY (*rising and moving* C) Then that's all right. I'm clear of the marrying for cash motive. That's how I like it. I should have felt uncomfortable if you'd said Betty had five thousand a year or even five hundred.

VICTORIA (*with genuine admiration*) That does you credit. I like independence and independent people. You're like me in that. In fact, you're very like me in many ways. I suppose that's why we've got on together.

HARRY. So you don't blame me for wanting to come into the family?

VICTORIA. How odd it sounds—"coming into the family". Life plays some queer tricks.

(BETTY *enters* L)

BETTY (*pausing*) May I come in, Mother?

VICTORIA. By all means, dear.

BETTY (*crossing to the armchair* RC) I hope I'm not intruding, but I was dying to see you, Mother, and to know what you had to say. Were you surprised?

VICTORIA (*quietly; trying to smile*) It was somewhat unexpected.

HARRY. Your mother's taken it very well, Betty. I haven't been told to clear out of the house, so I think it's approved. You're a good sport, Vicky.

VICTORIA. "A good sport." That must be very high praise from a man.

HARRY. Well, I'll join them in the other room. Leave you to explain a bit more to your mother, Betty.

(HARRY *exits* L. VICTORIA *faces down* R. *She almost breaks down, but manages to keep up appearances with difficulty*)

BETTY. Mother.

(VICTORIA *turns to look at her*)

(*She moves to Victoria*) You don't mind—about Harry and me, I mean?

VICTORIA (*bravely*) Mind? Why should I? He's a very charming man, and if you're in love with one another, what is there to be said?

BETTY. I hope you're not cross because we've been so secretive, but I was terrified of anyone guessing anything until I was quite certain in my own mind. You understand, don't you?

VICTORIA (*moving* C) Yes, I understand everything now. I'm a most successful business woman, but a mere child in some things.

BETTY (*moving* R *of Victoria*) Mother, I'm terribly sorry . . . Sorry for you, I mean.

VICTORIA (*pretending not to understand*) Whatever for?

BETTY. Don't let's pretend. I know how ghastly it must be for you. I wouldn't blame you if you almost hated me.

(*There is a pause*)

It may be Harry's fault. I don't know.

VICTORIA (*turning*) Don't blame Harry. You can call your mother a foolish woman for imagining vain things. (*She sits on the chair* R *of the table. She pauses*) Anyhow, it's nice to think of Harry coming into the family after all. (*She smiles*) Though hardly in the way some people expected.

BETTY (*moving* C) Then you'll wish us luck?

VICTORIA. Didn't Harry pay me the supreme compliment of being "a good sport"? I must go on being a good sport.

BETTY. And there will be no ill-feeling? I should hate to think . . .

VICTORIA. My dear child, I want to see you happy, and I think you will be.

(BETTY *sits on the left arm of the armchair* RC *and relaxes*)

We both know something we can't easily talk about, so we'll agree never to mention it or think about it again. (*Her tone changes to her business manner. She rises and goes to the desk*) And now, my girl, perhaps you'll be good enough to ask John, John Yardley, to have a word. He'll be somewhere around.

BETTY. Yes, I'll tell him. (*She rises, moves towards the door* L, *then stops*) But, Mother, do you still want to see the family tonight?

VICTORIA. Most certainly I do. That's why John's here, and all of you.

(BETTY *looks curiously at her, then exits* L. VICTORIA *crosses to the fireplace, looks in the mirror and smoothes her hair.*
JOHN YARDLEY *enters* L)

VICTORIA. Ah, John, so glad you've come. I wondered if it was convenient at such short notice.

JOHN (*moving* C) It's always convenient, Victoria, when you send for me. I'm the willing slave always at your command.

VICTORIA. That sounds as if I were a wretched dictator.

JOHN. Then let me say I'm the devoted admirer who comes at the beckoning of the lady's finger.

VICTORIA. That's better. You sound in good form tonight.

JOHN. Yes, *romance* is in the air. I've been hearing the news in there. Of course you know.

VICTORIA. If you mean about Harry's and Betty's engagement, yes. Harry told me a few minutes ago. (*She sits on the sofa*)

JOHN. Sly chap, isn't he? (*He sits in the armchair* RC) Just think of it. Making up to quiet little Betty without anybody knowing. I don't know how she's kept it so quiet. Girls usually let it out if they're running round with a man. I'll bet you had no suspicion.

VICTORIA. You're right. I had not.

HARRY. She's clever to keep it from her mother, especially one as sharp as you. It's been a very rapid friendship. Why, Harry's not been in the town long. He must be a fast worker.

VICTORIA. I think he is.

JOHN. He's a good bit older than your Betty, but that's the right way round.

VICTORIA (*quickly*) That's just what he said.

JOHN. He's right. The man should be a few years older; gives more stability, and women who marry a younger man often have an uncomfortable time later.

VICTORIA. *They* should be ideally happy, then, according to you?

JOHN. Oh yes. He's not every woman's fancy, but Betty hasn't gone about much, and she'll probably settle down and make one of those ideal domestic-minded wives. Just suit Harry.

VICTORIA. I hope so.

JOHN (*laughing*) Doesn't it just show you how gossiping folks can get things wrong? More than one has whispered your name and Harry's, just because you've been seen together and he's been coming here sometimes. The very idea. What they call putting two and two together.

VICTORIA (*thoughtfully*) And making the wrong number.

JOHN. That's very good. The wrong number. (*He rises*) Well, didn't I pooh-pooh the notion to you a week ago? You'd want a stronger man than Harry, apart from his age and all that.

VICTORIA (*slowly*) I suppose I would, when you come to think of it.

JOHN. You're too sensible to throw yourself away on any adventurer who comes along with smooth talk and charming ways.

VICTORIA. You give me credit for intelligence, John.

JOHN. Well, of course.

VICTORIA. This last half-hour has proved I have very little real intelligence. Oh, I know I'm successful, but the knack of making money in business doesn't necessarily mean you have good common sense. Lots of people have a flair for business, but are simply fools about everything else. (*She speaks with such feeling that* John *looks concerned*)

John (*moving nearer to her*) I think this affair of Betty and Harry Bateman has upset you. You've nothing against the man, surely? And I don't think he's short of money.

Victoria. Money? I don't care what money he has. (*She rises. Flaring up*) Money's very unimportant at times—peace of mind matters more.

John (*relaxing on the right arm of the chair* RC) Don't concern yourself, Victoria. It'll turn out all right. You've been upset at the suddenness of it, and I can't blame you. After all, Betty was the last girl we expected to get engaged.

Victoria. Why shouldn't she?

John. I mean, we'd got so used to Betty being—you might put it—the one left at home, that I suppose we thought she wasn't going to bother about a man.

Victoria (*moving* c) Shall we put it that I kept her so imprisoned in the house that she never had a chance like other girls?

John. You exaggerate.

Victoria. Oh no, I don't. That girl is thirty in a few weeks' time, and for ten years she's been a quiet, uncomplaining, general servant, without the servant's time off and days of liberty, and she's had no wages, just her keep.

John. You've not done it deliberately.

Victoria. Deliberately or not, I've done it, haven't I? I've made my own daughter work as the cheapest housekeeper in the country.

John. But it wasn't intentional.

Victoria (*moving to the fireplace*) A few weeks ago, when I was taking stock of myself and the family generally, I made her a gift of a hundred pounds. Perhaps conscience money for spoiling years of her life. She was like a child with its first ten-shilling note. (*She faces the audience*) She bought clothes, smart shoes, hats, and transformed herself into quite an attractive girl. I think that hundred pounds did the trick.

John. You mean it started Harry looking at her?

Victoria. Yes.

John. Then your money was well spent.

Victoria (*looking at him quickly; with a queer smile*) As a solicitor, you *would* say that.

John. Don't you?

Victoria (*slowly*) Well, of all my little gifts, it's had the most peculiar results.

John. She's going to get married. She'll be settled and happy. Stop bothering about how you've treated Betty in the past; that's finished. After all, you've been the means of getting her off with this fellow, so if you considered you'd kept her down a bit, you've made amends and brought these two together. What more can you want?

VICTORIA (*with a strange smile*) Yes, you've put it all in a few words, John. Anything I owed to Betty is paid in full. (*She relaxes and sits at the right end of the sofa*) It's a good thing I still have my sense of humour. It's a great help.

JOHN. That's one thing I like about you.

VICTORIA (*more light-heartedly*) Only one thing, John?

JOHN. Among the many others, my dear. (*He rises*) Now, Victoria, we've been talking about Betty and Harry. Let's have a change and talk about people more important—ourselves.

VICTORIA. Look here, I asked to see my solicitor tonight. Are you my solicitor, or are you a man who's taking advantage of his position . . . ?

JOHN (*moving to L of the sofa*) My dear, you do me an injustice. You asked me to call tonight. Why, I am not told. It's obvious it was *not* to hear the news of Betty's engagement, because you did not know that yourself half an hour ago, so I thought perhaps you wanted to see me purely personally, and you would even refer to what I asked you last week . . .

VICTORIA. Just like a conceited man. Can't I ask you up here without your getting absurd ideas into your head?

JOHN. Are they absurd?

VICTORIA. Well, most people would say they were.

JOHN. We're not bothering about most people. It's just the two of us. As I would say in court, confine yourself to the facts, woman.

VICTORIA. Don't call me "woman"!

JOHN. Very well—darling.

VICTORIA. I'm nobody's darling—yet.

JOHN. Oh, still hope, then? But you haven't answered me. Am I here tonight as a man or as a solicitor? Your answer is important.

VICTORIA. Shall we say you're here as a friend and solicitor rolled into one? John, I've come to a definite decision, and I want to make everything clear to my family.

JOHN. Victoria, before you tell me anything, and I feel sure you intend telling me of your plans, will you let me say a word? If I spoke afterwards, it may be too late, or you may think I'm pressing because of your decision.

VICTORIA. Very well, I'll listen.

JOHN. Good. (*He sits beside her on the sofa*) You'll remember, no doubt, I said a few words to you after the County Ball. Perhaps you'll even remember what I said.

VICTORIA (*teasing*) I think I can remember. It was only last week.

JOHN. Good grief! Whether it was last week or last year, you
D*

couldn't forget what I asked you. Now pay attention, Victoria. This is serious.

VICTORIA. Were you by any chance proposing marriage to me, John?

JOHN. Well, what do you think I was doing? You know perfectly well everything I said.

VICTORIA (*smiling at him*) I do. No woman forgets a proposal, even if it's made by an intoxicated man!

JOHN. I was absolutely sober. My regard for you is such that I'd never dream of coming into your company in that state, let alone talking to you.

VICTORIA. All right. I'm teasing again.

JOHN. You're not making it easy for me.

VICTORIA. Are you telling me that your proposal was made in all seriousness?

JOHN. I am. And what's more, I repeat the proposal. I'm asking you, Victoria, if you'll marry me.

(*There is a pause*)

VICTORIA. Forgive me, John, but you're not making this out of any feelings of sympathy, I hope?

JOHN. Sympathy? You don't need sympathy. Whatever made you ask me that?

VICTORIA. Oh, nothing. Forget what I said.

JOHN. As I told you last week, this is no sudden thought on my part. For years I've respected you and admired you, and never dared mention it. For one thing, you've been a busy woman.

VICTORIA. Too busy to think of marriage; why not say it?

JOHN. It's true; you were. But now even you admit such a thing is possible.

VICTORIA. You're a very shrewd man, John. I'll be frank with you. I even decided to marry again.

JOHN (*rising; in alarm*) Victoria, why have you let me go on like this? I've been making a fool of myself. I can see it all now. You've called the family together and made your plans, and to-night you're going to tell them you're going to marry.

VICTORIA. Am I?

JOHN. Well, am I not right? You admit you're going to marry again. It's all so obvious. (*He strides up* c) As your solicitor, may I be told who the lucky man is?

VICTORIA. I've no idea!

JOHN (*turning and staring at her*) I don't understand.

VICTORIA. You don't. The best solicitors don't jump to conclusions. They wait for evidence. Perhaps I shouldn't teach you your business.

JOHN (*moving slightly towards her*) Do you mean there's really nobody after all?

VICTORIA. I do.

JOHN. But you said you were going to marry again.

VICTORIA. That's right. (*She rises*) I'm open to offers. I'm what you call "on the market".

JOHN. Just what I was thinking.

VICTORIA. Oh, were you? Not a very polite thought.

JOHN. No, I mean that gives me a chance after all. Victoria, you've been playing with me long enough. I ask you for the last time, will you be my wife? (*He moves to her*)

VICTORIA (*moving to the fireplace*) As the modern girl would say, what do you offer me?

JOHN (*moving* c) Well, I've got a fine business connection. I'm not without money, you know.

VICTORIA. Money's nothing to me. I've probably more than you. (*She sits on the sofa*)

JOHN (*moving to* L *of the sofa*) Very likely, so money's no attraction. Then I just offer myself; perhaps not a very wonderful catch, but I could be worse. I'm no youngster, admittedly. I'm sixty, you know, but for my age I think I'm pretty good.

VICTORIA (*looking quizzically at him*) H'm!

JOHN. I can play golf with the best of 'em, I can manage a fifty-yard sprint, and even play a mild game of cricket still. And I'm no molly-coddler! Why, I don't wear those long underpants. Just look at my legs! (*He bends down to roll up his trousers*)

VICTORIA. Stop it! I don't want to see your legs! Men's legs are not pretty. They should be kept hidden!

JOHN. Sorry. I was only proving . . .

VICTORIA. I'll believe you. Tell me, John, do you snore?

JOHN. No. At least, I don't think so. And on the subject of sleeping, I might say I don't need a hot-water bottle. Wonderful circulation!

VICTORIA. That's nice to know. Most comforting. I'm a very cold person. Anything more?

JOHN (*sitting on the sofa beside her; quietly and sincerely*) Yes. Just my love and devotion to the end of my life. I will care for you and cherish you in the way you so richly deserve.

VICTORIA (*moved*) Thank you, John. I couldn't hear anything lovelier than that. You plead your case so charmingly, how can I resist?

JOHN. You will?

VICTORIA. Yes, John. I will.

(JOHN *takes* VICTORIA *gently in his arms and kisses her*)

JOHN. You've made me tremendously happy, my dear. I can hardly believe it's true.

VICTORIA. Neither can I. What have I done?

JOHN. You mean it, surely? You won't change your mind?

VICTORIA. No, John, I won't let you down.

John. And I won't let you down. My remaining years should be the happiest of my life. And I know they will be.

Victoria. I'll help you in making them so. (*Her tone changes*) Do you realize my family are waiting all this time to hear what I've got to say?

John (*smiling*) You've something quite different to say now.

Victoria. I don't think so.

John. But do you still want to meet them? Hasn't all this cancelled your plans?

Victoria. No. In fact my plans are based on my getting married.

John. But when you called them together you couldn't possibly know you'd have a proposal of marriage?

Victoria. Ah, I must have second sight.

John. You're an amazing woman.

Victoria. Yes, I amaze myself sometimes. (*She rises and moves to press the bell at the upstage end of the mantelpiece*) You realize, John, you'll have to come and live here?

John. I'll live anywhere with you. (*He rises*)

(Hetty *enters up* LC)

Victoria. Oh, Hetty, please ask my family to come in here, will you?

Hetty. Yes, Mrs Anson.

(Hetty *exits* L)

Victoria. And you can bring that fearful animal of yours with you. I don't like bulldogs, but if I have you, I suppose I'll have to suffer your dog as well.

John. You'll love him, Victoria, and he'll love you.

Victoria. I'll be content with your love.

(William *enters* L, *followed by* Sally, Robert, Betty, Harry *and* Peter. Victoria *moves* C *to welcome them*)

Victoria. Come in and sit down somewhere. Sorry I've kept you so long, but we've had business to discuss.

William (*moving to the armchair* RC) We've filled in the time nicely, Vicky.

Victoria. And nearly emptied the bottles, I expect.

William. You must be a clairvoyant.

(Betty *and* Harry *sit on the sofa.* Peter *sits on the pouffe by the fireplace.* Victoria *sits on the chair* R *of the table and* Sally *sits* L *of the table.* Bob *sits on the chair at the desk* L *and* John *moves down* R *to the armchair and sits*)

But we had a solemn duty to perform, that of toasting the newly-engaged couple here. I wouldn't ever have it said an Irishman didn't do the right thing at a time like this. Such a surprise it was; our little Betty, the quiet little mouse!

VICTORIA (*rising*) Yes, the quiet mouse often captures the cheese.

WILLIAM. There now, Harry my boy, you're likened to a piece of cheese. (*He laughs*) Where was the old cat?

VICTORIA. Father, if you've finished your untimely remarks . . .

WILLIAM A thousand pardons, my dear!

VICTORIA. What I'm going to say won't take many minutes, but it should interest you all. Recently I was reminded by my father —the old rascal—and by Robert, that time was going on. So I planned drastic changes, and here they are. I should say that tonight extraordinary things have been happening, which I hadn't expected, but, curiously enough, I can carry out my original intention . . . (*She pauses, then sits* R *of the table* LC) I am going to retire from active work in the firm.

(*There is a general gasp from them all*)

BOB (*rising*) Mother, you can't mean it!

PETER (*rising*) I say, Mother . . .

VICTORIA. Boys, please don't pretend. It's what you wanted, and it's right. I'm going to divide the firm into four parts; one for Betty, one each for you boys, and one part for myself.

BETTY. Oh, Mother, I'm no business woman.

VICTORIA. You won't need to be. Your husband will look after yours. He's a very good business man. (*She looks at Harry*)

BOB. Do you mean that we all share in the profits?

VICTORIA. Precisely. Robert, you will be managing director; Peter will be general manager.

(BOB *moves to Sally, and puts an arm round her shoulder*)

You will each have an increase in salary befitting your position.

PETER. I say, this is marvellous! It's terrific! Perhaps I can get married now.

VICTORIA. You must. I make that a condition, as I want you out of this house. You'll marry within three months, and I'll give you two thousand pounds to help start your new home. Will that suit?

PETER. Will it suit? I'll say it will! (*He turns to John*) Mr Yardley, does she mean it?

JOHN. She does mean it, and I'm a witness for you.

PETER (*moving to Victoria and kissing her*) Mother, you old darling! Would you mind very much if I dashed off to Pauline this instant to tell her? (*He hugs Victoria*)

VICTORIA. Don't fuss me. Go and tell her if you must, you impatient boy.

PETER. Excuse me, everybody!

(PETER *rushes up to the door* LC *and exits*)

VICTORIA. To resume. Robert, you and Sally should have a home of your own. A young married couple should not live with in-laws. It may not have occurred to you, but I hope you agree.

BOB (*looking at Sally*) Yes, Mother, we do.

VICTORIA. Then the quicker you go the better. Like Peter, I give you three months to clear, and set up your own home, and I provide three thousand pounds to help the start of it.

SALLY. Oh no, I can't believe it!

BOB. Mother, it's too exciting for anything! A home of our own and all that money. I don't know what to say. I'm stuck for words.

WILLIAM. For a man who's speechless, you're blatherin' a lot.

BOB. But it's generosity beyond all reason.

WILLIAM. Never question generosity, my boy. Just accept it as sent from Heaven above. And now let's have a bit o' quiet, as I'm all ears for the rest.

(SALLY *rises. She and* BOB *move up towards the door* L)

VICTORIA (*rising*) Betty darling, it's usual for a girl in your position to have an allowance, and I'm sorry to say I'm guilty of omitting that in the past; so to make amends, I'm making you an allowance of two hundred a year. I'm sure Harry can provide some luxuries, but that will be all your own.

BETTY. Thank you, Mother.

VICTORIA. If my family think I'm generous, it is perhaps due to pangs of conscience. You've all served me well, and I made up my mind to do something in return. (*She pauses, then sits*) This has suddenly struck me like the reading of a will. It is rather like it, isn't it? But what a thrill to me to make these gifts while I'm alive and can see the pleasure you will have from them.

WILLIAM (*fumbling in his pocket and drawing out a handful of loose change*) You've done your family proud, Vicky, and no mistake. It must be nice to be one of your chicks. Instead, I'm just your rascally old father, who doesn't deserve to be thought well of.

VICTORIA. You don't, and I'm glad you know it.

WILLIAM. When you were talkin', I was thinkin' what a grand feelin' it must be to have presents o' that kind showered on you. But the likes o' them are not for such as me. Never mind. (*He rises*) I'll go on tryin' to make ends meet on my miserable allowance, and my generous heart will still have love for you, even if your generosity has limits.

VICTORIA. Last, but not least, I come to you, Father. You are not forgotten. It's high time you gave up living in those rooms. You must drive that poor woman off her head, so you'd better come and live here.

WILLIAM (*not pleased*) You mean I give up my independence?
VICTORIA. You're not independent. I pay your debts.
WILLIAM. There won't be room for me in this house.
VICTORIA. Oh yes, there will. You can have Robert's two rooms.
You'll save all the expense of living away, and in addition I'll
give you an increased allowance; only a small increase, but it will
be useful.
WILLIAM. Well, I don't mind that arrangement. I might even
benefit by it. I take it, now you've lifted the Prohibition clause on
the house, you'll keep to it like a decent Christian?
VICTORIA (*laughing*) You'll be all right.
WILLIAM. Then I come, Vicky, my darlin'. (*He turns to Betty*)
Oh, Betty, you'll have to come sometimes and see as your mother's
treatin' me fair. There'll only be the two of us . . .
VICTORIA. Three.
WILLIAM. Just you and me, you said, as the others are going
away.
VICTORIA. Just you and me and John. (*She rises*)

(HARRY *and* BETTY *rise*)

BOB. What's this? Mother, are you going to marry . . . ?
JOHN. Yes, Bob. Your mother's going to marry me.
BETTY (*moving to Victoria and kissing her*) Oh, Mother, this is
lovely, and I'm so glad it's who it is.
JOHN. Thank you, Betty.
BOB. So am I. I couldn't have chosen better for Mother if she'd
left it to me.
HARRY. Congratulations, Vicky. (*He shakes Victoria's hand*) As
children can't choose their fathers, perhaps they should be
allowed to choose their step-fathers. (*To John*) She's a fine woman,
John.
JOHN. I've known that for years.
WILLIAM (*moving down to* L *of John*) So you're the nigger in the
woodpile. And have I got to share the house with a man like
yourself?
JOHN (*rising*) So Victoria says, and she's the boss.
WILLIAM. I might have known there was a snag in it.
VICTORIA (*moving to William*) What's the trouble?
WILLIAM. Law and order. If there's anythin' more upsetting to
an Irishman it's law and order. He's the law, isn't he? If ye must
marry again, Vicky, why in the name of the Saints have ye to
choose a solicitor, a man of the law?
BOB. That's fine, Grandpa. We get free advice now.
WILLIAM. So we do. I hadn't thought of that, my boy.
JOHN (*whispering in William's ear*) I might be useful to you one
day when you're caught in a certain place, after time.
WILLIAM (*alarmed*) Ssh! Never speak of such things. Vicky,

perhaps you've not done a bad thing after all, and you have my blessin', both of ye.

VICTORIA. Thank you, Father.

WILLIAM (*moving* c) Well now, what's the use of a blessin' if you don't do it in a fitting manner? Let us perform a solemn duty, and toast the couple who are once again embarking on the troubled sea of matrimony! Suppose we go and have that solemn toast? Come on now! (*He moves to the door* L) I'll be host as I'm now livin' in this house!

(WILLIAM *exits* L, *followed by* BETTY, HARRY *and* BOB)

SALLY (*moving to the door, then pausing*) Thank you for all you're doing for Bob and your grandson.

VICTORIA. There she goes, John, reminding me I'm a grandmother!

(*A baby's cries are heard.*

　　SALLY *grimaces and exits up* LC. JOHN *and* VICTORIA, *left alone, stand looking at each other and smile*)

VICTORIA. Well, the great ordeal is over. (*She moves to the fireplace and pokes the fire*) Facing my family is like going into a witnessbox. (*She sits at the right end of the sofa*)

JOHN (*sitting beside her*) You've done magnificently for them. What a mother!

VICTORIA. I've discovered that giving makes me happy. I feel happier than I've ever felt before. And after all that orgy of giving, I'd better deal with you, John.

JOHN. What am I in for?

VICTORIA. A lot of fussing and petting! Isn't that what you like, what all men like, in fact?

JOHN. That's it. Do you know, my dear, I'm reminded of something I heard on the radio? They called it *Life Begins at Fifty*. That's you, you're starting afresh.

VICTORIA (*rising and moving* c) John darling, I'm really excited as if I were twenty-five. That's how it should be, isn't it? And we're going to have many happy years together and we'll live to be a hundred.

JOHN (*rising and moving to Victoria*) Yes, my dear. And using the poet's words, I say to you in all sincerity, "Come, grow old along with me, the best is yet to be . . ."

　　He kisses her as—

the CURTAIN *falls*

FURNITURE AND PROPERTY PLOT

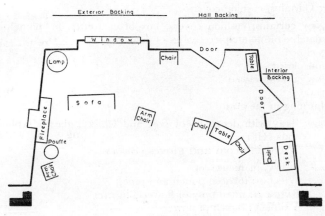

ACT I

On stage: Table (LC). *On it:* books, magazines
2 chairs (R and L of table LC)
Desk. *On it:* inkstand, pens, pencils, blotter, neat piles of papers,
bills, etc.
Chair (by the desk)
Chair (R of door up LC)
Sofa. *On it:* cushions
Armchair (RC)
Armchair (down R)
Mirror over mantelpiece
Curtains at the window
Light switch L of door up LC
Standard lamp
Occasional table
Doors closed
Window closed
Window curtains closed
Lights on
Fire burning in the grate

Personal: ROBERT: cigarettes, matches, notecase containing bank-notes
PETER: lighter, cigarette-case with cigarettes, loose change in overcoat pocket
VICTORIA: bundle of papers and bills
WILLIAM: pipe, watch on chain

ACT II

Strike: Curtains, cushion covers
Set: New curtains, cushion covers, box of cigarettes on mantelpiece, matches on mantelpiece, vases of flowers
Doors closed
Window closed
Window curtains closed
Lights on
Fire burning in the grate
Off stage: Tray with decanters of port and whisky, glasses, syphon of soda (HETTY)
Victoria's coat and gloves (BETTY)
Personal: BETTY: manicure set
WILLIAM: tobacco pouch and pipe
BATEMAN: small posy of flowers, lighter
YARDLEY: bunch of flowers

During CURTAIN fall:
Strike: used glasses from tray, empty decanter
Set: clean glasses and full decanters on tray

ACT III

Strike: Vases of flowers
Set: Fresh vases of flowers
Doors closed
Window closed
Window curtain closed
All lights on
Fire burning in the grate
Personal: SALLY: sewing
PETER: cigarettes and matches
WILLIAM: loose change

LIGHTING PLOT

Property fittings required:

    Fire in grate, practical
    Standard lamp, practical
    Centre light (or wall brackets), practical
    Light switch L of door up LC
    Bell push above fireplace

Interior. The same scene throughout.

ACT I

Evening. Winter
Fire burning in the grate
Standard lamp and centre light lit

ACT II

As for ACT I

After the CURTAIN fall:

    Take out all lights except the standard lamp
    Bring up fire glow

Cue 1. VICTORIA switches on the centre light
        VICTORIA: As you say, "What's the harm?" (Page 35)

ACT III

As for Act I

8ſ